Hollywood Costume Design

by

Travilla

Maureen Reilly

Schiffer Publishing Ltd

4880 Lower Valley Road, Atglen, PA 19310 USA

Library of Congress Cataloging-in-Publication Data

Reilly, Maureen E. Lynn.
Hollywood costume design by Travilla / by Maureen Reilly.
p. cm.
ISBN 0-7643-1569-2 (hardcover)
1. Travilla, William, 1922-1990. 2. Costume designers--California--Los Angeles--Biography. 3. Hollywood (Los Angeles, Calif.) I. Title.
TT505.T73 R45 2003
791.43'026'092--dc21
2001011477

Designed by Bonnie M. Hensley
Cover design by Bruce M. Waters
Type set in Rage Italic LET/Lydian BT

ISBN: 0-7643-1569-2
Printed in China

Published by Schiffer Publishing Ltd.
4880 Lower Valley Road
Atglen, PA 19310
Phone: (610) 593-1777; Fax: (610) 593-2002
E-mail: Schifferbk@aol.com
Please visit our web site catalog at www.schifferbooks.com
We are always looking for people to write books on new and related subjects. If you have an idea for a book, please contact us at the above address.

This book may be purchased from the publisher.
Include $3.95 for shipping.
Please try your bookstore first.
You may write for a free catalog.

In Europe, Schiffer books are distributed by
Bushwood Books
6 Marksbury Avenue
Kew Gardens
Surrey TW9 4JF England
Phone: 44 (0) 20 8392 8585
Fax: 44 (0) 20 8392 9876
E-mail: Bushwd@aol.com
Free postage in the UK. Europe: air mail at cost.

Dedication

For my children, John and Jamie,
who have learned to love old movies.

Travilla

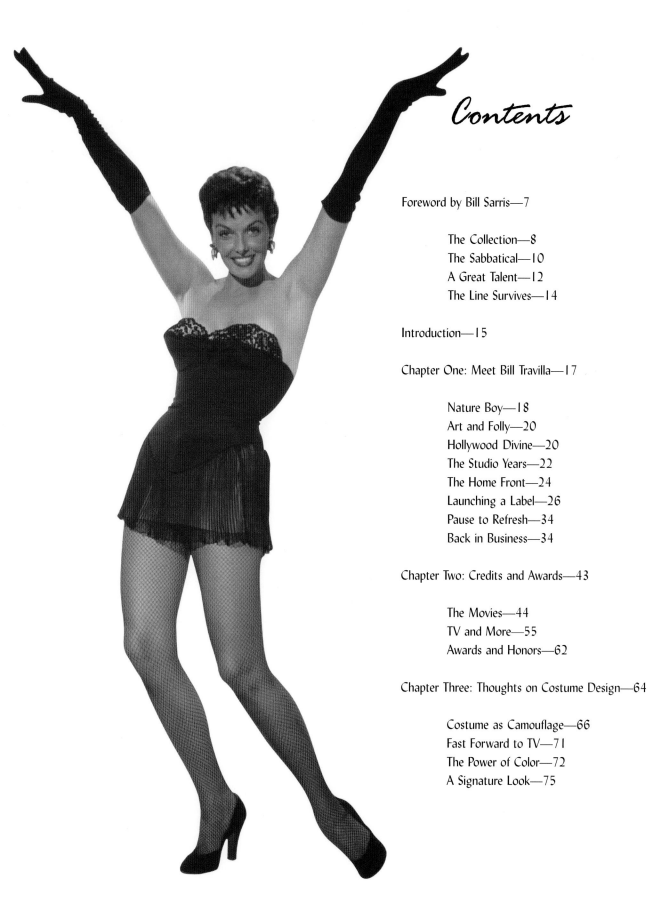

Contents

Foreword by Bill Sarris

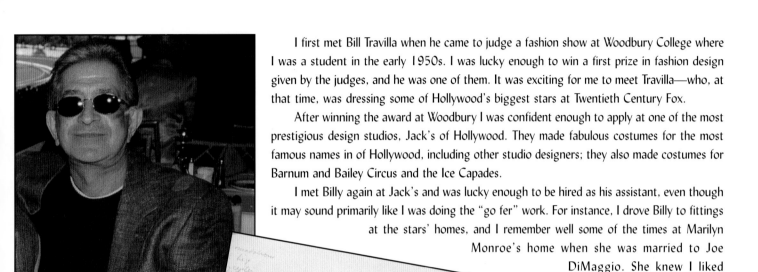

I first met Bill Travilla when he came to judge a fashion show at Woodbury College where I was a student in the early 1950s. I was lucky enough to win a first prize in fashion design given by the judges, and he was one of them. It was exciting for me to meet Travilla—who, at that time, was dressing some of Hollywood's biggest stars at Twentieth Century Fox.

After winning the award at Woodbury I was confident enough to apply at one of the most prestigious design studios, Jack's of Hollywood. They made fabulous costumes for the most famous names in of Hollywood, including other studio designers; they also made costumes for Barnum and Bailey Circus and the Ice Capades.

I met Billy again at Jack's and was lucky enough to be hired as his assistant, even though it may sound primarily like I was doing the "go fer" work. For instance, I drove Billy to fittings at the stars' homes, and I remember well some of the times at Marilyn Monroe's home when she was married to Joe DiMaggio. She knew I liked shrimp cocktails so she'd fix me one herself. Now, it was just pre-cooked shrimp and bottled sauce, but the point was she made it with her own hands! Marilyn had a reputation as being difficult with the brass, but she was wonderful with the little people like me! You know, for years Billy would never admit that he had an affair with Marilyn, but I knew they were very close. He never confided in me, even though I was as close to him as anyone; he was very private. But apparently he admitted to the affair just before his death.

I became very much the assistant to Bill and traveled with him whenever he went to do fittings with the big-name stars. One time we went to see Dorothy Dandridge in Las Vegas when she was wearing a gown Bill had designed. He was known for his work for her nightclub acts. Afterward, Billy invited her to come out and have a drink with us. She said, "You know they won't let black girls like me in the lounge." So she invited us both up to her rooms and we had our drinks there. She was really a great lady.

Bill Sarris, snapped in the late 1990s.

A white cocktailer designed by Travilla for Dorothy Dandridge. *Collection of Bill Sarris.*

There was really a big change in the motion picture industry about this time. Television was rearing its ugly head and motion picture studios were laying off their contract players as well as all their designers and other production staff. It was, in its way, a tremendous revolution in the industry.

It was about this time that I started to talk to Bill about going into business together. I'm still surprised that I had the confidence to suggest it to him, because even with as much time as I spent with him I sometimes realize how little I actually knew about him. He was a very private person and never went out for the Hollywood social scene.

So there you are. We worked, traveled, and hung out together but I didn't know much about him personally. I just knew that he had great talent and if he could make women beautiful on the screen, why not in their private wardrobes? It just seemed to be the right timing to open his couture business.

Talk about dumb bravado! We didn't know anything about the retail industry. Didn't even know you could buy ready-made dressmaker dummies. We made our own, padded to the sample size. We didn't know how hard it was to crack this crazy business. It was Bill's sheer talent that made it take off.

When Bill left Fox in 1956, the business really began to grow. It was a private label, but marketed as ready-to-wear. Anyway, it didn't take long for the movie stars, who knew Billy from the studios, to discover they could have beautifully designed clothing in their personal wardrobes. But this still wasn't enough and Bill kept his hand in show business by doing freelance work for movies, theatre, and television. Few TV viewers will forget Loretta Young sweeping into her introductions on *The Loretta Young Show* wearing his gowns.

Probably his greatest talent was being able to take any woman and make her look more beautiful. Bill's years in Hollywood most likely formed this ability to see the best in any woman. Not every star was a beauty, but Bill was able to enhance just the right characteristic...and make her look like one.

One of Travilla's earliest sketches for his own collection, of a cocktail dress with classic lines. *Collection of Bill Sarris.*

In a town of incredible talent Bill stood out as one of the great designers of his day, whether for women or men. He was able to enhance even Errol Flynn, Clark Gable, Richard Burton, and Marlon Brando—all of whom had great, natural presence.

Now Bill's talent wasn't just confined to beautiful clothing design. His own oil paintings were just as spectacular. He also took up photography as a hobby and produced some amazing pictures on a trip to Africa.

Bill Sarris poses with Julie Sommars at a fashion show featuring the wardrobe Travilla designed for her role in a TV series, *The Governor and J.J.* Collection of Bill Sarris.

The Sabbatical

You'd think that, given all the years we were associates, I'd have understood how Bill thought. But it came as a tremendous shock to me when suddenly, after successfully running "Travilla, Inc." for decades, he just up and quit! This was back in 1971. On what seems like a whim, he took an ocean liner to Malaga, Spain. I drove him to the docks; we were both living in New York at the time. It seemed like a crazy thing to do, but I could see that he was tired and I guess he needed the time.

We closed the business. I stayed in New York for a couple of years when suddenly I got a wire from Billy saying, "I'm ready to go back to work!" He went to work for Neil Diamond (the designer, not the singer) for a couple of years. Then, in about 1976, we started the business again.

The silk Travilla label.

A Gallery of Design

Some of Travilla's most glorious work seems to have sprung from his sabbatical in Spain. In the early 1980s, after renewing his business, Travilla produced vibrant, glowing gowns that are so classic in design they could be worn today.

Travilla's working sketches are remarkably detailed, so that each stands on its own, like a portrait. Of course, he also did quick pencil sketches on tissue paper, but the final production sketches are beautifully finished in watercolor on thick, creamy 10" by 16" posterboard. This gallery of sketches for his own line, circa 1980, speaks a mute testimony to his genius as a designer *and* as an artist (*All, collection of Bill Sarris*).

Top right, bottom right: Lettuce-hemming swirls up the torso, on a pair of scotch-and-soda ballgowns.

Another sensational gown, this time a ruffly whirl of printed chiffon.

Two printed chiffon hostess gowns, with an ethnic edge.

A golden glow of luxury fabric for elegance after five.

A delirious rose-skirted ballgown, each petal stiffened by wire.
A delicious pinked *peignor*, each scallop boasting lacy cut-outs.

A Great Talent

Bill got credit for most of the clothing he designed, but I'm still steamed over the fact that he never gets credited for that halter-top dress worn by Marilyn Monroe in *The Seven Year Itch*. He did get a movie credit, but in the big book on Hollywood costume design by that so-called expert Diana Vreeland, it was listed as having been purchased "off-the-rack."

Off the rack! This was in the 1950s and the studios didn't buy *anything* in those days. It was all custom-designed, right down to a work shirt. My buddy designed the most famous dress in the world and he deserves full credit for it. As you probably know, the publicity boys took a still from the movie, showing Marilyn standing over a subway grating so that a blast of air caught her skirt. They blew it up to gargantuan size and made a poster of it to show over the movie marquee—and that image has been shown over and over again, all over the world.

The most famous dress in the world, designed by Travilla for Marilyn Monroe to wear in *The Seven Year Itch*. United Press International.

Talk about larger than life! Because that's how Billy was, in his great talent. It's still hard for me to believe he died the way he did, so suddenly. We were interrupted one day at work—I remember Bill was fitting a gown—with a message from his doctor.

Turns out Bill had lung cancer; he got the diagnosis by telephone. It was just like him that he kept on working that day and for weeks afterward. But he died within the next three months. I really think it was the chemotherapy that killed him.

Bill had very little ego but I was with him on one of those last hospital visits when a nurse approached to help. Bill wasn't looking his best, and to this day I bless that nurse, because she said he reminded her of Clark Gable and it really cheered him up.

A candid shot of Travilla at play in the 1980s. *Collection of Bill Sarris.*

The famous nude calendar on which Monroe penned a personal, rather teasing note, asking Travilla to "dress me forever." Collection of Bill Sarris.

The Line Survives

After Billy's death, I just kept the line going with designs by Paul Whitney. That worked out really well, because he'd been working for us under Bill's direction for almost a year so he already knew the line and the concept. When Paul left in 1993, I hired Lourdes Chavez, and today David Paley designs the collection. As always, it's distributed through boutiques and specialty stores nationwide.

We moved to South Grand Avenue a few years ago after a fire at our old workrooms on East Seventh Street. That fire was a real disaster, not only from the business end of things but because so many of Bill's original sketches were destroyed. I saved all that remained, trying to preserve them. I still have several dozen.

I also kept Bill's design awards, and there are plenty. You know, the usual procedure is for a designer to nominate himself for an Oscar or Emmy, but Billy never did. It's not that he was too modest, since he was always thrilled to be recognized. It may have been a matter of pride—he couldn't stand the Hollywood types who were always asking for favors—or it may have been tied up with how he avoided putting himself into the public spotlight. Fortunately, someone else always nominated him!

Personally, my favorite memento is the calendar of Marilyn where she posed in the nude on red velvet. That's the one she autographed "To Billy, my love. Please dress me forever. Love, Marilyn." I know that inscription by heart.

Bill used to have it hanging over his fireplace. After he died, I had it blown up about a hundred times. Now it's hanging in the dining room of my home. Once again it's an image that's larger than life, just like he was.

Introduction

This is a story about art and artistry, friendship and folly, fashion and film. It's the story of Hollywood costume designer William Travilla, who cloaked Marilyn Monroe and a score of other legendary screen beauties in the looks we know and love.

Travilla and his wife Dona Drake in the 1960s. *Collection of Bill Sarris.*

A young Travilla, working hard at a movie studio sketchboard. *Collection of Bill Sarris.*

Travilla saw the best of the twentieth century, and helped define part of it. Born on March 22, 1920, he died on November 2, 1990 at the age of seventy while still actively running his own business as a private-label designer. He'd spent all of his adult years, and much of his youth, in what could easily be termed a larger-than-life screen role.

Just before he died Travilla was planning to publish his memoirs under the working title *Tigers I Have Known*. His notes, and a cache of press clippings, were saved by his long-time friend and business partner Bill Sarris. This material has been a fresh and personal source of research. It's as if Travilla was able to speak again, more than a decade after his death.

Ultimately, Travilla's story is a richly visual one that would be impossible to tell without ample reference to the sketches and photos of his work. It's rare for such ephemera to have been preserved in the garment industry or in Hollywood, where the historical value of clothing is only now being recognized. Thankfully, Sarris saved dozens of Travilla's original sketches, and they form the heart of this book.

Note: For more information on this subject, see "A Take on Travilla," in the author's earlier book California Couture (Schiffer Publishing, 2000). There, the focus was on Travilla's private-label business; here, it is on his work as a costume designer.

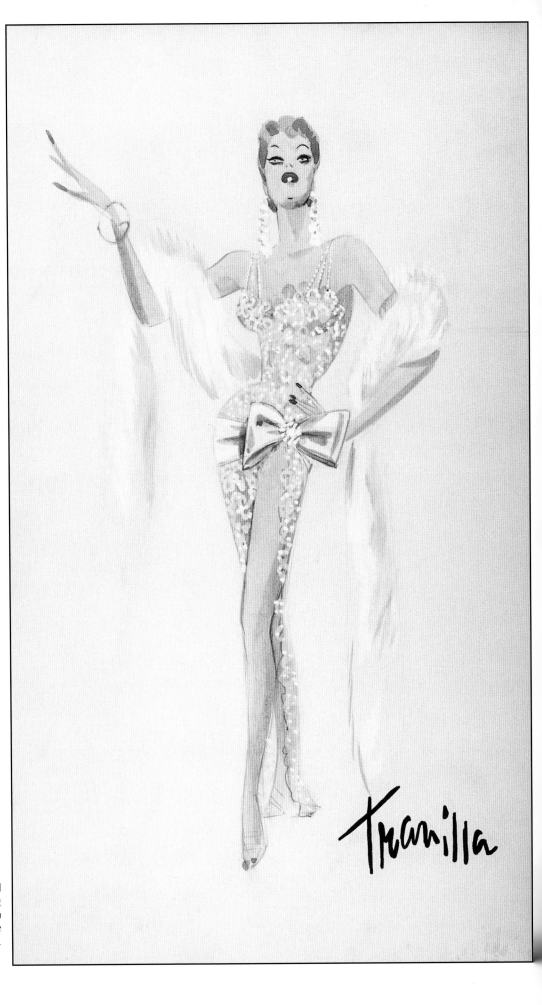

As always, Travilla sketched the actual likeness of the person he was designing for—in this case movie star Debra Paget, possibly for *Bird of Paradise* (1951). Collection of Bill Sarris.

Chapter One

Meet Bill Travilla

It was 1920, and the world was about to roar into the Jazz Age. That same year, William Travilla was born and raised on Catalina Island off the coast of Southern California. The island was notable for its isolation and wild beauty. It was, and is, accessible only by boat—about an hour away from the trendy restaurants and tourist shops in San Pedro and other beach towns.

He was the son of Bess, a beauty of half-French and half-Chinese ancestry, and Jack Travilla, of Spanish descent. Sadly, he would never know his natural mother, as she died from complications surrounding a second pregnancy when he was only about a year old. From the age of three Travilla was raised by his father's second wife, Ruth.

It was this formidable lady who recognized his talent and insisted that he receive art training—over the wishes of his maternal relatives, who thought the violin more suitable for a young boy. His sister Joan, born nine years after him, remembered her mother's stories about his precocious behavior. "As a six-year-old, he'd stop her in a store and point to a lady, saying what a pretty dress she had on. Then he'd sketch it."

Ruth wasted no time and enrolled him straightaway in the prestigious Chouinard School of Fine Art, where he was recognized as something of a prodigy. As Travilla himself remembered: "After a few terms I was too advanced to stay in the children's class. They put me in an adult class, although I was still only eight. The move up meant I studied sculpting but it also meant I was part of the live-model class where nude men and women posed for us to draw. It only came to the attention of my family when I told my grandma about a lovely red-haired model we had drawn in class, and how she had lovely red hair 'down below' as well!" His grandmother was horrified, and said he needed lessons in music, not art.

"She went out and bought me a violin and brought it over to our house. But then it was my stepmother's turn to be furious. She grabbed the violin and broke it over her knee, before throwing the pieces back at my granny. From then on, there was no question but that I would continue in art school."

Travilla posed with his younger sister Joan Garlow on the boardwalk in San Pedro, circa 1940. Catalina Island, and its round Art Deco casino, is visible in the distance. *Collection of Bill Sarris.*

Travilla sketched these evening gowns in 1937, when he was about fifteen years old. *Collection of Bill Sarris.*

Travilla studied at Chouinard until he was fourteen, and thoroughly sick of his regular schooling. "I was allowed to continue art school providing I put in four hours a week at other studies, but all I wanted to do was draw."

Initially, Travilla had aspired to be a sculptor. He was encouraged in this by his father, an art lover who spent his spare time in Europe, haunting the museums. But when Travilla was in his late teens, he realized sculpting would be a long and expensive road to financial independence, and so he began studying commercial art at Woodbury College in Los Angeles.

Nature Boy

When Travilla reminisced about his childhood, however, it seldom concerned art lessons. Instead, he would call forth images of how he ran wild on Catalina Island, where his father and two uncles worked as stunt divers and champion swimmers. He grew up on a house high on a hill overlooking the island's bay with its yachts, steamers, and pleasure pier.

As a young boy, Travilla spent hours by himself playing wild Indian in a rocky cove not far from home. Later, he would dive for coins thrown by tourists from the docks of Avalon, the only town on Catalina. "I used to joke that I should have gone into the swimwear business, instead of designing evening gowns," he said.

Travilla was always intrigued by the wild side, as expressed in this early sketch dubbed "Savage" (production unknown). *Collection of Bill Sarris.*

A later sketch, also exotic, shows a maturing in style. The notation "Cleopatra" indicates this was possibly designed for *Princess of the Nile* (1954) starring Debra Paget. *Collection of Bill Sarris.*

His father, famed for holding the long distance underwater swimming record, had taught Travilla to swim almost as soon as he could walk. Jack Travilla's underwater swim of 126 yards in two minutes, thirteen seconds still stands as a record. Two of Travilla's uncles and his paternal aunt were also famous swimmers and held national championship records.

His father and two uncles worked in vaudeville and took their act to Europe on the Orpheum Circuit. "I still have a poster where my father and his brothers are billed above Eddie Cantor as The Travilla Brothers with their diving act and their three seals."

"I grew up surrounded by water. As a boy, the island was really rugged; when I hiked into the interior, it was like stepping into my own private world of adventure." This carefree childhood was to change abruptly when his father suffered a serious accident on stage.

"He split his head open. He couldn't dive any more, so we moved to the mainland where he ran a tire store. But I was always an islander, and when I was in my early teens I would go over to Catalina for the summer and make enough money to be able to rent a little room there."

It was a fifteen minute ferry ride from the trendy restaurants and shops of San Pedro to Catalina, where tourists could enjoy the island's grand neo-classical casino. The teenage Travilla would dive for coins thrown by the winners from the docks of the pleasure pier. He also worked for one of his uncles who had a glass-bottomed boat.

"It was about the size of a large rowing boat, with glass in the middle and seats all around so people could peer down into the sea. My job was to stay out beyond the kelp gardens where the undersea life was so beautiful." Once his uncle had rowed to a pre-appointed spot, Travilla would swim beneath the boat and perform stunts such as peeling and eating a banana underwater.

Art and Folly

Headstrong and independent, Travilla was just fourteen when he refused to continue with his regular schooling. "All I wanted to do was draw. My father agreed that I could cut back, if I worked for him in the mornings and went to art school in the afternoons."

That was the plan, but Travilla was often waylaid. It seems he had to pass by the old Follies and Burbank burlesque houses on the way to class, where he was drawn into the bump-and-grind shows that fascinated him.

It may be that Travilla came to show business naturally, given that his maternal aunt Sybil was a silent film actress and her husband Jules Furthman was a screenwriter—not to mention his father's life in vaudeville. In any event, he was an instant hit with the ladies of burlesque.

After he got to know several of the strippers, who must have been bemused by the attentions of such a young fan, he told them that he would redesign their costumes. By now Travilla was sixteen, and was running a brisk little business selling pencil sketches to the strippers—at a bargain rate of three for a flat five bucks.

It was a strange career path that Travilla took, from artless nature boy to artistic boy wonder. He took a detour along the way when his grandfather left him a $5000 legacy. "Both my grandmother and stepmother urged me to invest the money, but I was young and fancy-free," he said. "I knew exactly what to do—spend it!"

He was about eighteen when he and a cousin traveled for almost a year throughout the South Seas, with a long layover on the island of Tahiti. Their trip took place just before that part of the world would be closed off to travel by the outbreak of World War II in the Pacific. On his return to the states, the draft-age Travilla was declared 4F due to flat feet.

Hollywood Divine

Now Travilla began working for Western Costume, ghost-sketching for costume designers at the studios that produced the Hopalong Cassidy and Tom Mix series. From there, he went to Jack's of Hollywood, a production company that rented and sold costumes to many of the major movie studios.

He was ghost-sketching again. "Designers who could not draw well used to come into Jack's to rent a costume and I'd make a sketch of it. They'd ask me to alter the neckline, or some minor change.

"I worked hard and did some beautiful drawings for them; but what I discovered was that they were simply signing their names to my sketches and taking them back to the studios, and showing them to the producers for approval."

Travilla took it all in stride. "It was good basic training for me," he said. "I had great fun going to see these movies and learning from all the mistakes, without having to take credit for them." He learned well, and applied his ideas to a series of sketches for ice skating champion Sonja Henie when she came to Jack's to have costumes made for a spectacular new ice show.

"She had her own famous designer [at Jack's] . . . but I made some sketches and to flatter her I put her face on my drawings," Travilla recalled. He knew that her regular designer sketched with a lot of flair, but no real detail. "When you looked at the garments in his drawings, you didn't know what was going on."

He watched Henie from a corner of the fitting room, when she came in for a consultation with her regular designer, whose sketches were laid out on the floor for approval. "After poring over them, Sonja decided she hated them. I watched her vent her disapproval by treading all over them, even kicking them!"

That's when the boss asked her to take a look at some drawings that one of his young designers had done. He introduced Travilla, of course, and Henie loved his work at first sight.

It was an important commission. This type of success, and some prodding by his friend Bill Sarris, inspired the young Travilla to make a first stab at running his own business.

"I ended up buying a share in Jack's with grand ideas that I could please all the great designers of Hollywood . . . who could get their costumes made there," he said. "But it didn't quite work out.

"Jack's excelled at doing costumes for the circus with a staple machine and glue, throwing on a feather here and a sequin there. I had a very different dream I wanted to pursue."

While still at Jack's of Hollywood, Travilla designed for United Artists and Columbia Pictures, as well as a number of small independent studios. But he was disappointed by the general run of film assignments, and decided to start an independent costume company, called 'The Costumer.' "The idea was that I would meet the need for quality designs by working with the other [studio contract] designers."

Travilla could only speculate as to why his plan did not meet with success. "There seemed to be a jealousy among all these so-called designers and they would only come to see me as a last resort," he said. "I suppose they didn't want another designer seeing all their drawings in case they were copied."

A sketch of Garbo as *Camille*. Since her costumes were designed by Adrian for the 1936 MGM movie, this may have been a classroom exercise. *Collection of Bill Sarrís.*

1860

An early sketch of an Incan maiden. Her scanty costume and towering headdress resonate with the look of burlesque. *Collection of Bill Sarrís.*

The Studio Years

Like so many other young men in their early twenties, Travilla was not inclined to be patient. If only he knew that, by a trick of fate, he was about to launch his career as a contract designer for the movie studios. Indeed, Travilla was about to go on contract with the prestigious Warner Brothers.

It all hearkened back to his impulsive fling in Tahiti, where he "learned how to do the hula and how to get along with the native girls." He also painted, and came back inspired to paint semi-nude native beauties, on black velvet. "OK, so it sounds corny, but they were something new at the time."

He began selling these oils at the gift shop in Don the Beachcomber's, a popular Hollywood restaurant. The actress Ann Sheridan liked to eat there and she bought several of his oils to redecorate her boyfriend's apartment. One night when Travilla was at the restaurant, she asked to meet him.

"The manager called me over. I could hardly believe what I was hearing, but I rushed right over! Ann and I hit it off straight away. We just clicked. Then and there, she became my Aunt Annie."

When Sheridan asked Travilla to comment on the dress she was wearing, he was glad to offer suggestions. As he remembers their conversation, she suddenly said: "Your ideas are so clever. If the studio wants me back on my own terms, and they will, then you are coming with me as my designer."

It was 1945, and Sheridan was world-famous thanks to her publicity by Warner Brothers as the "Oomph Girl." A striking redhead, she was often cast as the girl with the smart remark, and she had already wisecracked her way through a string of movies with James Cagney, Humphrey Bogart, and Ronald Reagan.

Now in her fifth year of contract, Sheridan was demanding star privileges and had just walked out on negotiations at Warner Brothers. When the studio acquiesced, she was true to her word to Travilla. "The studio called me in," he said. "Suddenly I was working on A movies—all her movies were Grade A—and I was earning $400 a week."

Sheridan continued to promote her favorite designer until Travilla was under contract, with a ten-week guarantee at $1,000 a week. Quite apart from the money he was earning, it was the break of a lifetime.

He worked with Sheridan on the big-budget *Nora Prentiss* (1947), a real fashion vehicle for which he won immediate acclaim. His next assignment was *Silver River* (1948), set in the aftermath of the Gold Rush. Travilla styled Sheridan as a grand lady with grit, wearing lace and silk in one scene and denim in another.

Travilla's work on *Silver River* appealed to Sheridan's leading man, Errol Flynn. When Flynn was cast in *The Adventures of Don Juan* (1949), he disliked the original designer's work, which was true to period with lace collars and doublet hose. Flynn said "not for old Dad" and demanded Travilla for a re-make of his entire wardrobe.

Costuming the swashbuckling Flynn in a vest and tights, rather than doublets and hose, Travilla set a trend that would be followed in dozens of adventure epics to follow. *Don Juan* garnered Travilla the first of many Academy Award nominations, and his only Oscar.

Travilla shows a selection of bonnets to a starlet, dating from his days at Warner Brothers. *Collection of Bill Sarris.*

Travilla and his Aunt Annie, in her dressing room on the *Silver River* set. *Collection of Bill Sarris.*

An original sketch for Sheridan's role as a mine owner in *Silver River*. *Academy of Motion Picture Arts & Sciences.*

Flashback to Travilla's stint at Jack's of Hollywood, where he first met his wife, Dona Drake. She was a new starlet in town who'd come to Jack's to have some clothes made for a movie. "It really was love at first sight for both of us," Travilla said. "She was just 20 years old and she'd already beaten Betty Grable for the title of 'leading pin-up of the year' so you can imagine . . . "

They married just ten days after they met, at City Hall in Santa Monica. "Dona wore a plaid cotton shirt and a pair of Levis, with a bandanna as headdress. I bought her an orchid corsage. Even in that get-up, she was a beautiful sight to behold."

When they first met, it was Drake who had the more promising career. Following a stint in vaudeville as "Rita Rio," the leader of an all-girl band, she landed a contract with Paramount Pictures. She was often cast in exotic roles—beginning with her first film, *Aloma of the South Seas* (1941) starring Dorothy Lamour.

It was love at first sight for Drake and Travilla. *Collection of Bill Sarris.*

Dona Drake during her glamour girl heyday. This is before she married, when she led an all-girl band under the stage name "Rita Rio." *Collection of Bill Sarris.*

The beautiful brunette worked with Lamour again in a Hope-Crosby classic, *The Road to Morocco* (1942). Drake's other film credits include *So This is New York* (1940s) with Rudy Vallee; *Beyond the Forest* (1949) with Bette Davis; *Without Reservations* (1946) with John Wayne; and *Valentino* (1950), in which she learned to dance flamenco.

"But let me tell you, it's not so easy being married to a celebrity," Travilla would complain. "Dona had enough of a fan club following, for the studio to deliver her mail in great bags to our house. Fans were always calling and pestering; if we went anywhere in public, even to the beach or a movie theater, soon there were a few kids tailing us, and then a crowd. You don't have much privacy."

Drake did not place much stock in her own career. "She thought the husband should take care of the wife," Travilla laughed. "I'll never forget, we were just married when her agent called and said he had secured a three-week personal appearance for her in Las Vegas at $5,000 per week. Dona said, 'I'm not going anywhere. I've got a husband and he's going to take care of me.' Not only did I see $15,000 and a good vacation slipping away, but it also meant I had to work!"

As Travilla soon learned, Drake suffered from a form of epilepsy, and it was partly for this reason that she often refused a casting call. But there were also emotional difficulties, insofar as Drake tended to so immerse herself in a role that it created difficulties for both husband and wife.

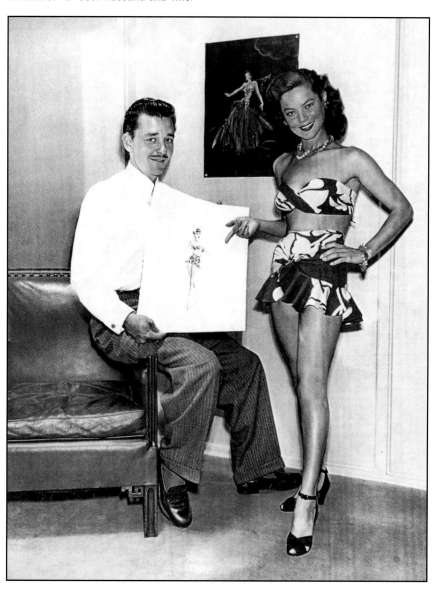

Drake posed in a brief sarong costume designed by Travilla, possibly as a freelance assignment for her role in *The Road to Morocco* (1942). Note his oil-on-velvet painting in the background. *Collection of Bill Sarris.*

As he put it: "I often worked with Dona. Early on, I designed for a few of her films, including *Princess of the Nile*. Later, she would sometimes model for my collections. But she was one of those actresses who . . . found it hard to come home and step out of the character she'd been playing all day."

The couple were together for twelve years before they separated, and they stayed married until Drake's death in 1989. Their daughter Nia, who was born three years into the marriage, came to live with Travilla when she was sixteen years old, at a time when her mother was having emotional problems.

Shortly after Nia moved in with him, they had dinner with a neighbor who was also the wife of a major film producer. As Travilla recalled, with some trepidation: "Virginia Zanuck took one look at my daughter, and wanted to give her a screen test! Of course, Nia was all for it, but I put on the brakes."

His reasoning was simple, and heartfelt. "Given Dona's problems, and the heartache that I saw so many screen beauties go through as they grew older, I advised Nia to stay out of show business. She took up a career as a veterinarian—so I guess she thought my advice was pretty good after all!"

Travilla's beautiful daughter Nia, as a teen. She inherited her father's love of water sports. *Collection of Bill Sarris.*

Launching a Label

In 1952, Twentieth Century Fox wooed Travilla from Warner Brothers. He stayed for just four years, during which time he worked on eight of Marilyn Monroe's movies. He wryly called himself "the king of cleavage" thanks to his reputation for turning out sexy showgirl costumes, but he really wanted to design elegant clothing.

Putting the final touch on Sheree North's costume for *How to Be Very, Very Popular* (1955). Travilla excelled at over-the-top showgirl looks. *Collection of Bill Sarris.*

In 1956, when Fox declined to renew his contract, he was glad to go. It was at a time when budget cutbacks were causing an end to in-house costume designers at all the studios . . . it was the end of Hollywood's golden era.

When the cuts came, the enterprising Travilla was well poised to take flight. After all, he'd already been freelancing on a regular basis, along with designing special-event gowns and a limited line of private-label clothes. Leaving Fox gave Travilla the time he needed to turn his venture into a full-time business.

Many of his first customers were the stars who had learned to trust his judgment when he'd created a special look for their entertainment roles. Why couldn't he work the same magic for their personal wardrobes?

Fussing over a coat and dress ensemble on Joanne Woodward, possibly for *Signpost to Murder* (1964). Travilla convinced her to break her usual mold of tailored blouses and full skirts, in the movies and in life. *Collection of Bill Sarris.*

For his own label, Travilla devoted himself to creating elegant, couture-quality clothing. He was often lauded for the dignity and beauty of his designs, especially when contrasted with the outrageous trends that seemed to dominate the mid- to late-1960s. His philosophy was to bring out a woman's natural allure as "the female of the species, uncertain, unpredictable . . . a feminine approach that drove men crazy for centuries."

Feminine looks to drive men crazy, from the late 1960s. These evening styles make good use of vermicelli beading, lace, and chiffon. *Collection of Bill Sarris.*

Travilla

Travilla also showed great style for day, as in these sketches from the 1960s and 1970s. The peasant dress is especially appealing. *Collection of Bill Sarris.*

Spiral bands of
Broadtail –
Every other used
in reverse to
effect high light
+ shadow.

These mini-length coats from the mid-1960s have luxury detailing, as revealed in the sketch notes. *Collection of Bill Sarris.*

Nutria mated to
leather

Travilla

Through it all, in spite of the romance and glamour, Travilla remained an artist who needed to refresh his creative spirit. In his case, that meant traveling to exotic lands at every opportunity. "I really grew up appreciating nature. It was the beginning of my love for the primitive and for wild animals," he reflected.

Although Travilla often traveled at the end of a showing season, in 1971 he went on a lengthy sabbatical from the world at large. It was after he'd tried, without success, to move his workrooms to Puerto Rico. "I was getting to a period where I felt I couldn't truly trust people, and the women at this time were not really wearing my clothes. They were into Levis and doubleknit pantsuits, not my cup of tea."

Demoralized, he shut down the workrooms and moved to New York. There, he lived in a suite at the Gotham Hotel with his own private menagerie, two kittens and a macaw, for company. "I was nuts to live in a hotel and I didn't like New York either. I was despondent and lonely, but I stuck it out for nine months—until I looked in the window of an Italian shipping line and saw a poster of the sea, and blue skies."

That's when Travilla packed his entire household—kittens, bird, and all—and took an ocean liner to the remote village of Malegna in Spain, where he had friends. "I was sick of the way women were dressing, in blue jeans and any old thing. It seemed like the concept of fashion had come and gone. So I went."

While in Spain, Travilla relived his beach bum days on Catalina Island, but he realized it couldn't last forever. "I could have lost my perspective and not known where I belonged in the world, if I had stayed too long." The final impetus for his decision to leave came when he noticed that women were starting to dress stylishly again. At first, it seemed that "the girls just as shabby as in America; most were in jeans." When he saw them wearing skirts and dresses, he decided it was time to come home to high fashion.

Back in Business

After a hiatus of at least four years—accounts differ as to how long he was gone—Travilla returned stateside, seeking work in Los Angeles. He hoped to renew his business right away, but settled for a job with the designer Neil Diamond for an interim period.

He also picked up freelance work in television, beginning with the ambitious three-part special *Moviola*, which chronicled the life of Marilyn Monroe and other major stars. Then it was the movie *Cabo Blanco*, shot on location in Mexico.

By the mid 1980s, when Travilla was hired by Lorimar Productions to re-design the leading lady wardrobes on the TV series *Dallas*, he and Bill Sarris had the business up and running again. For Travilla, this just meant further opportunities to travel. His wanderlust did not start, nor end, with the Spanish sojourn.

Travilla had always traveled to Europe on business—fabric-buying expeditions and the like—and continued to do so now. For pleasure, he visited Egypt, Syria, and the South Seas. He also e undertook at least two camera and painting safaris in Africa.

Opposite page: This intriguing composite shows a photo of native dress and a sketch of the cocktailer it inspired for Travilla's collection. *Collection of Bill Sarris.*

Travilla

Two of Travilla's oil paintings, inspired by his stay among the Masai. *Collection of Bill Sarris.*

Unlike the average tourist, Travilla did not stay at a decent hotel and merely trek about the African country with a guide. Instead, he lived with the Masai tribe, eating their food and sleeping in their huts. As with all his trips, the African experience not only refreshed Travilla's soul, it inspired his next clothing collection.

This ethnic-print patio dress was designed for Diahann Carroll to wear in her television series *Julia. Collection of Bill Sarris.*

The dress on the opposite page was directly inspired by Travilla's stay among the Masai tribe in Africa, when he went on camera safari. *Collection of Bill Sarris.*

A bevy of African-inspired evening looks for Travilla's
private label collection, dating to the late 1970s.
Collection of Bill Sarris.

Travilla died in 1990 following an unexpected diagnosis of lung cancer. Now his free spirit was released forever, leaving behind a legacy that has yet to be fully realized.

In life, Travilla was a modern day adventurer who wanted to experiment with new ideas, explore new territories. "Did you ever hear of Jean-Pierre Hallet?" he once asked. "If I were anybody else I'd want to be him —writer, adventurer, explorer, anthropologist."

In reality, Travilla was all that, and more.

Travilla at his most debonair, in a publicity portrait from the 1960s. *Collection of Bill Sarris.*

Chapter Two

Credits and Awards

An early showgirl costume by Travilla (production unknown). Collection of Bill Sarris.

1939

Elizabeth and Essex

1941

The All American Co-ed

1942

Two Yanks in Trinidad
White Cargo (+Robert Kalloch)

1943

The Desperadoes
Redhead from Manhattan
Two Senoritas from Chicago
The Woman of the Town

1944
Ever Since Venus

1946

The Verdict
The Beast with Five Fingers
Love and Learn
Night and Day

1947

Nora Prentiss
The Unfaithful
Cry Wolf (+Edith Head)
Escape Me Never (+Bernard Newman)
That Hagen Girl
Always Together
My Wild Irish Rose

These test shots of *The Unfaithful* (1947) show why Ann Sheridan was called the "Oomph Girl" at Warner Brothers. *Collection of Bill Sarris.*

April Showers
Silver River (+Marjorie Best)
Good Sam
Two Guys From Texas (+Leah Rhodes)

For *April Showers* (1948), Travilla put Ann Sothern in a charming period gown. *Collection of Bill Sarris.*

WARDROBE TEST
FOR
"APRIL SHOWERS" 688
OF
ANN SOTHERN
AS
JUNE TYME
WARDROBE CHANGE #21
WORN IN { SET INT. DAY COACH UNFINISHED
SCENE 115-117
10-2-47
SC. #
TAKE #

1949

The Adventures of Don Juan (+Best, Rhodes)
Flamingo Road
Look for the Silver Lining (+Best)
Dancing in the Dark
The Inspector General
When Willie Comes Marching Home
Mother Didn't Tell Me

1950

The Gunfighter
The Daughter of Rosie O'Grady (+Best)
Panic in the Streets
No Way Out
Mr. 880
I'll Get By
American Guerrilla in the Philippines
Rawhide
Woman on the Run

1951

David and Bathsheba (+Edward Stevenson)
On the Riviera (+Oleg Cassini)
Half Angel
Take Care of My Little Girl
Meet Me After the Show
The Day the Earth Stood Still (+Perkins Bailey)
The Pride of St. Louis
Viva Zapata!

1952

She's Working Her Way Through College (+Best)
Lydia Bailey
Dreamboat (+Renie)
Don't Bother to Knock
Monkey Business
Bloodhounds of Broadway
The Farmer Takes a Wife

Two designs for starlet Dorothy McGuire in *Mother Didn't Tell Me* (1949), as featured in a *California Stylist* article from August 1950. The dress has satin-faced wing lapels and black net over a column of green satin.

1952 (cont'd)

Down Among the Sheltering Palms
Powder River
Pickup on South Street

The Girl Next Door
King of the Khyber Rifles
Man in the Attic
I Don't Care Girl

The harem look, as interpreted by Travilla for Ginger Rogers in Dreamboat (1952). It features a whaleboned top in copper satin with silver lamé pants, and a lavish overskirt. *Collection of George P. Erengis.*

Mitzi Gaynor tests her costume for the *I Don't Care Girl* (1952). The gowns
were memorable, the film was not. *Collection of George P. Erengis.*

1953

Gentlemen Prefer Blondes
White Witch Doctor (+ Dorothy Jeakins)
How to Marry a Millionaire
Pickup on South Street
The Farmer Takes a Wife
Down Among the Sheltering Palms

1954

River of No Return
The Rocket Man
Princess of the Nile
The Raid
Garden of Evil
Broken Lance
The Gambler from Natchez
The Black Widow
There's No Business Like Show Business (+Miles White)
White Feather
Hell and High Water
Three Young Texans

1955

The Seven Year Itch
How to Be Very, Very Popular
The Left Hand of God
The Tall Man
Gentlemen Marry Brunettes (+Christian Dior)
The Rains of Ranchipur (+Helen Rose)
The Lieutenant Wore Skirts
The Bottom of the Bottle

Jane Russell at her most covered-up, in *The Tall Man*
(1955). She played the survivor of an Indian attack, with
Clark Gable as a renegade Confederate soldier. *Collection
of Bill Sarris.*

1956

1957

The Revolt of Mamie Stover
Twenty-three Paces to Baker Street
The Proud Ones
Bus Stop
The Bottom of the Bottle

The Fuzzy Pink Nightgown

A dramatic gold hostess gown for Jane Russell's role in *The Fuzzy Pink Nightgown* (1957). Travilla also designed a baby doll nightie, true to the title. *Motion Picture Academy of Arts and Science.*

1960

1963

1964

From the Terrace

Mary, Mary
Take Her, She's Mine
The Stripper

Signpost to Murder

This pale coat with mink collar topped a matching tunic dress with mink skirt, as worn by Diane McBain in *Mary, Mary*
(1963). The same outfit was featured in Travilla's line for Fall 1963 where it retailed for $695. *Collection of Bill Sarris.*

Joanne Woodward is devastating in a frothy black-and-white evening shirtwaist, attributed to *Signpost to Murder* (1964). Travilla also sketched an all-black stunner for the same film. *Collection of Bill Sarris.*

JOANNE WOODWARD
#3
"SIGNPOST TO MURDER"

Travilla

1967

Valley of the Dolls

1968

The Secret Life of an American Wife
The Boston Strangler
Daddy's Gone A-Hunting

1969

WUSA

1979

Cabo Blanco

Travilla chats with Sharon Tate. She wears a camel coatdress he designed for her role as the doomed Jennifer in *Valley of the Dolls* (1967). *Collection of Bill Sarris.*

TV and More

In the 1960s and 1970s, Travilla worked as a freelance designer for a number of TV shows and specials. He found television a difficult medium, as compared to movies. "It's done so hurriedly. In [film] I'd have the actor or actress eight weeks before the shooting started. With television, I'm lucky to get them three days ahead of shooting."

Travilla also designed nightclub engagement gowns and personal appearance clothing for Cyd Charisse, Dorothy Dandridge, Mitzi Gaynor, Judy Garland, Lena Horne, Julie London, Marilyn Monroe, Deborah Paget, Debbie Reynolds, Ginger Rogers, Kay Starr, Connie Stevens, Connie Francis, Nancy Wilson and many others. His specific television credits are listed here.

Ann-Margret specials
The Big Cube
Dallas
Diahann Carroll specials
The Dinah Shore Show (selected segments)
She's Dressed to Kill (fashion show)
Evita Peron
The Governor and JJ
That Hagan Girl
He and She
The Jacqueline Bouvier Kennedy Story
Julia
Julie London specials
Knots Landing
The Loretta Young Show (entrance gowns)
Movieola (all three segments)
My Wicked, Wicked Ways...The Legend of Errol Flynn
A Sreetcar Named Desire
The Thorn Birds

A special-event gown sketched by Travilla for Marlene Deitrich, one of his personal film idols. *Collection of Bill Sarris.*

MISS ANN MARGARET
Las Vegas

Travilla

Two dynamic costumes for Ann-Margret. *Collection of Bill Sarris.*

Miss Kay Starr, in concert. *Collection of Bill Sarris.*

A froth of pink for
Connie Stevens. The
lettuce-edged hem
of her tiered skirt is
stiffened with wire,
a Travilla trademark.
*Collection of Bill
Sarris.*

A slink of ink for
Connie Francis,
employing another
Travilla trade-
mark—the bias cut.
*Collection of Bill
Sarris.*

MISS CONNIE FRANCIS

rhinestone bodice worn
with Black cage skirt
over narrow slim skirt.
Top skirt embroidered
with rhinestones in a
rain pattern —

Travilla

669
Lena Horne

Travilla

This Grecian gown complements Lena Horne's classic beauty. *Collection of Bill Sarris.*

Awards and Honors

Travilla was nominated for an Oscar several times, including *How to Marry A Millionaire* (1953), *There's No Business Like Show Business* (1954), and *The Stripper* (1963). But he only took home the golden statuette for his work on *The Adventures of Don Juan* (1949).

He was also richly recognized for his work in television. His first Emmy nomination came in 1978 for a fashion show sequence in *She's Dressed to Kill*. In 1980, he received the award for *Movieola*, a three-part series that included a review of Marilyn Monroe.

Travilla was nominated for an Emmy every year thereafter, for four years running: *Evita Peron* (1981), *The Jacqueline Bouvier Kennedy Story* (1982), *The Thorn Birds* (1983), and *A Streetcar Named Desire* (1984). He captured the trophy in 1985 for his work on *Dallas*, and was nominated the next year for his second season on that series.

Travilla with one of his Emmy awards.
Collection of Bill Sarris.

SC 115-156
Hyannisport - meets
Kennedy Family, plays
touch football

This outfit was
designed by
Travilla for *The
Jacqueline
Bouvier Kennedy
Story*. It
captured the
quintessential
Jackie, all casual
elegance. (Soft
pink was one of
her favorite
colors.)
*Collection of Bill
Sarris.*

Travilla

Chapter Three

Thoughts on Costume Design

A movie personality is not born, but produced; and costume design is a critical component in the process. Even Marilyn Monroe, who built her *persona* on the disarming notion that she might shed her clothes at any moment, is remembered best in the clothes that were designed for her by Bill Travilla.

He was her lover and close friend as well as her designer. He preferred to caress her body with silk and satin, to create a living valentine. Yet he could also garb her in cheap black rayon as the role demanded in *Bus Stop*; and in simple white terrycloth for a girlish bathtub scene in *The Seven Year Itch*.

Travilla put men in tights when he deliberately took liberties with period dress for Errol Flynn's role in *The Adventures of Don Juan*. But he also put men in skirts, as when he dressed Danny Kaye in mock drag for *The Inspector General*.

WARDROBE TEST FOR "HAPPY TIMES" 8194 OF DANNY KAYE AS GEORGI WARDROBE CHANGE # 7 WORN IN SET INT MAYOR SEC SCENE 102-106 KOSTER 6-30-48 HALLE SC.# A92 TAKE # 1 CAMERA D2

Danny Kaye hammed it up, even for costume tests.
These were for his many roles in *The Inspector General*
(1949). Collection of Bill Sarris.

Travilla could be subtle, designing a black cocktailer with deep darts at the neckline that echoed the way Joan Crawford clawed her way to the top in *Flamingo Road*. Or broad, as when he garbed Joanne Woodward in little more than a metaphor, with strategically placed paste and fringe, for *The Stripper*.

Here was a designer who brought out the aura of an actor or actress, and polished it white-hot for the galaxy of stardom. With Travilla, it was a matter of natural talent. "There are no rules when it comes to costume design," he said.

"Every person is different and maybe my approach is totally different from other designers. They probably went to art school, learned pattern drawing and sketching, and were *taught* to design. Personally, I don't think that's something you can teach. I think that's a talent that you either have or haven't got."

The process began with reading the script. "At home I study it [the script] and think about the character I am dressing. I have to ask myself: 'What kind of person is she really?' Then I write down how many scene changes there are for the actress, and little memos about whether the scene is day or night, interior or exterior.

"Next I go and talk to the director and ask what he thinks of the character. Then I talk to the actress to get her views, and then it's back to my office to start sketching. Generally, my [initial] drawings are 90% on target."

"As a rule, I expect to be respected as a designer when I'm working on a film the same way I respect an actress or actor. I don't try and tell them how to act, and I don't expect them to tell me how to design. I demand respect."

Costume as Camouflage

Travilla reflected on why the studios considered it so important to have a costume designer assigned to each star during the golden era of Hollywood. "The answer is that if you take a beautiful woman who is also a magnificent actress and photographs wonderfully for the cinema—odds are, she will not also have the perfect body.

"The designer's job, in most cases, is to flatter her. Even though the role she might be playing is not a *fashion* role, the designer is still going to make her look great. To do this . . . the designer uses camouflage.

These test shots for a young Zsa Zsa Gabor (production unknown) show Travilla's penchant for glamour. *Collection of Bill Sarris.*

"With camouflage, I can make an actress who is heavy look taller or thinner. You don't want anyone in the audience thinking the actress is too fat, or short-waisted. There are illusions the designer can use . . . to make the actress more glamorous.

A fine example lies in the few designs he made for his beautiful wife, the actress Dona Drake. She was dark and striking, but very petite. Travilla used tailoring tricks, making small changes in the scale of a collar and the proportion of a skirt, to give her a longer look.

"In those days, the designers were under contract, four or five to a studio. Sometimes we were handling three movies at a time. We made sketches for approval, then we made the clothes, then we had them photographed—both for still and moving camera shots—and then we studied them, and with pencil lines kept on improving them. Expense was not the issue."

This sketch from the early 1950s uses a guitar prop, enhancing the look of a Spanish singer. The flowing, fluid fabric acts to elongate the figure, an aspect of camouflage. *Collection of Bill Sarris.*

The same process was used to make the male actors more handsome. As with Erroll Flynn, who would change the collar on a costume a dozen times and then declare: "Oh, oh. We were better off the way we had it before." Likewise, Travilla recalled, Gary Cooper would try on fifty hats before he found one he liked.

Then there was Clark Gable, who always asked for costumes with black shirts "because he thought [they] made him look a little more sexy and swarthy." Tony Curtis was such a perfectionist that Travilla declared him "a pain in the neck to work with," and Charles Bronson was just plain rude.

Jason Robards is the perfect gentleman in a double-breasted suit by Travilla (production unknown). *Collection of Bill Sarris.*

"He & She"
Safari jacket
of Cheeta - breed
in leather

A sketch for the television series *He and She*, which featured Richard Benjamin in the male lead. *Collection of Bill Sarris.*

Golden boy Robert Redford glows in a Travilla design (production unknown). *Collection of Bill Sarris.*

"These people weren't wrong or they wouldn't have been where they were," he admitted. "But they could be just as finicky as actresses." Only Richard Burton was easy to please. "All he ever said was, 'It's OK, Luv.'"

Travilla said it best when he spoke about creating authentic Mexican peasant costumes for *Viva Zapata!*, one of his favorite projects. "There is a time when you can be Pygmalion as a designer for the movies because you are not only doing the clothes, but developing the character. It can be thrilling to create one person into someone else."

Fast Forward to TV

When Travilla began working in television, he found it to be a different world from the movies. There was still the need to bring out an actress's best features and make her glamorous, but the pace was much faster and the budget much smaller.

Using *Dallas* as an example, Travilla spoke of television's collapsed shoot schedule. "That's where the hard work came in. We were producing a show each week, and they needed new costumes for the stars *plus* the supporting cast. Even the extras, depending on whether it was an important scene.

"Unlike the movies, where costumes were always custom-made for a star, sometimes we had to buy from the racks. We also used garments from a prior show for the supporting cast and extras, which was actually true-to-life," he reflected. "Most people don't have a brand-new outfit to wear every day, not even the very rich.

"Here's another difference: the power of television as a visual tool. I think it's even greater than the movies. With *Dallas*, my clothes were seen immediately, every week, all over the world."

There was one thing that did not change for Travilla in designing for the movies as compared to television, which was his need to monitor how the clothes were *worn* during a given shoot. "A designer has to keep an eye on the set. I watch every time there is a wardrobe change, or an establishment shot. If there is a big scene coming up then I want to see everyone on the set because you have to keep a balance throughout.

"The leading lady, for example, might be in a scene wearing a black suit with a small white collar and the scene might work beautifully when she is in an office and when she is being walked to a car," he said. "But then there might be a scene coming up where a secretary, a bit player—someone I haven't dressed, someone dressed by wardrobe – happens to be wearing a little black dress with a white collar. Suddenly you have two people looking alike on screen, and you would have to send the extra back to be re-dressed.

"It may sound obvious but everyone who walks on that set has something to do with the other person. You have to be very aware. Mistakes can easily be made, and you often see them in today's [TV] shows because there has not been enough time, not enough thinking."

A purple dress like this would have been pivotal to color mapping on the set of *Dallas. Collection of Bill Sarris.*

The Power of Color

Color was of special use to Travilla, as a design tool. "A designer can use it to help the actress deliver her dialogue. Let's say we have a scene in *Dallas* where Sue Ellen is meeting JR and the audience knows from a previous scene that she is lying. Here you can affect the audience with color, an olive green or one of the off-colors.

"Now, if the script called for Sue Ellen to be truthful and sincere then I'd put her in white or pink, colors that are virginal and clean. If it called for passion, I'd use orange or red for a character like Sue Ellen."

Travilla had an instinct for using olive green to impart mistrust, as he described in detail for *The Boston Strangler*: "Tony Curtis was the central character and was never to be trusted throughout the whole movie. So I put him in tones of olive or dirty green—a distrusting color, the color of dead leaves.

"Color was so important throughout that whole film because it was one of the first movies to use multiple shots on the screen. That made it like a gallery of paintings and I had to try to not make them jar. So if I had a scene with men playing pool, followed by a bum on a street leaning against a brick building, then a scene with men in dark suits, followed by Tony Curtis sneaking through the bushes—there were several distinct colors. Billiard green, brick, navy blue and leaf green, to name a few.

"To give it all the impression of olive green, dirty green—I had one of the men wearing a green tie, not the same shade as the billiard table in the preceding scene, but more mottled. Then I put the bum on the street in a green scarf and dirtied with snow before he put it on."

A streetwalker costume, attributed to *The Boston Strangler* (1968), makes use of that untrustworthy green. *Collection of Bill Sarris.*

Tony Curtis
"Boston Strangler"
3 - 9 - 11

Travilla

These "working class" outfits in dingy colors were designed to make Tony Curtis look menacing in his role as the strangler. *Collection of Bill Sarrís.*

Albert De Salvo
"Boston Strangler"
Tony Curtis
1 ♦ 7

Travilla

another idea for style 662--- i,m still looking
for a pale watery print chiffon, but also thought
the gown could be lovely of kind of bronzy pleated
silk chiffon over emerald chiffon . the jeweling
at the empire waist of topaz, gold, and emerald.

another idea for style 662--- i,m still looking
for a pale watery print chiffon, but also thought
the gown could be lovely of kind of bronzy pleated
silk chiffon over emerald chiffon . the jeweling
at the empire waist of topaz, gold, and emerald.

Tramilla

The choice of color also had practical implications. "The characters have to blend in color-wise, and not fight each other. For example, you might have a scene in a nightclub where the leading lady is dressed in gold and you have 25 extras. If an extra comes on wearing gold too, she has to be re-dressed.

"You also have to make sure there aren't too many brilliant colors in the background. If your star is going to be seated on a red sofa, you certainly don't put her in a red suit—you have got to find definition.

"There may be five or six characters in a scene and if you have a color theory going in one particular area, and you know that Character Two will be walking over to Character Six, you have to be aware that they must complement each other. It's the designer who has to get these things right because no one else will be thinking these things through for you."

A Signature Look

Apart from the showgirl costumes he was famous for, Travilla strove to achieve a classic look. This was partly as a reflection of his own taste in clothes, and partly a matter of staying power. "Even in the olden days, I soon realized that my clothes had to last," he said.

"A movie then took maybe six months to shoot, then another six to edit, promote and release. Then it ran for two years or more," he tallied, "so it had to look good for around four years." Travilla felt the quickest to become dated were the hats, so he tried to eliminate them whenever possible. "I also simplified the accessories, that way my clothes would last."

Like any designer, Travilla had a signature look. In his case, it was pleating. "I love working with pleats because they do what *they* want," he said. "If you listen to what pleats are doing, then you can make a dress that truly fits." In fact, he was so well known for designing with pleats that he once quipped: "When I die, I don't want to be buried or cremated, just pleat me."

Another favorite technique was the bias cut, which made clothes that are subtle and move beautifully. "On the bias, fabric becomes much more difficult to handle because it has its own way of wanting to fall," he said. "But if you understand how it will fall, you can *create* with it. The fabric subtly leans into the body, touches the body, and is very aware of who is wearing the cloth. It's a very sexy look."

When Travilla combined pleats with a bias cut, as he often did for Marilyn Monroe, it was costume history in the making. "The gold lamé dress I made for Marilyn in *Gentlemen Prefer Blondes* was all done with two pieces of circular lamé wrapped on the body to a bias back seam.

"All the pleats measured exactly, there were no darts and no side seams." The fit was perfect, and so close that Monroe had to be sewn into it. Her other, even more famous pleated dress from *The Seven Year Itch* was also cut on the bias, which allowed the crepe fabric to flow like silk. (The fabric was dyed down from white to ecru, so that it would photograph white with the camera technology of the day.)

Travilla cut with such precision, he was known as an "engineer" of fabric. He often used hidden wires to fit a plunging neckline or create a permanent ruffle. His skirts seemed to move with a life of their own, whether they were made from layers of petals or waves of lettuce-edge ruffles or tiers of beaded vermicelli.

As with his mastery of color, so Travilla's ability to create movement in fabric hearkened to his training in classical art. He put it this way: "The color balance and the lines that I think into fabric are all part of a composition, which you could also call a painting.

"To me, composition is lines of beauty. Just as I score on a canvas where the sweep will be, I do the same on a fabric." Unlike a painting, of course, costume design had the added element of role-playing. This was not just an artistic process, but a dramatic one.

Opposite page: A swirl of pleating flows from a jeweled empire bust. This spectacular ballgown is described in Travilla's sketchboard notes as "kind of bronzy pleated silk chiffon over emerald chiffon." *Collection of Bill Sarris.*

The fireworks gown was modeled by Dorothy Malone, in this publicity shot from 1968. *Collection of Bill Sarrís.*

The same gown was featured on Barbara Parkins during a segment in *Valley of the Dolls* (1967) where she works as a top model. *Collection of Bill Sarrís.*

Travilla, master of the showgirl costume, was equally at home applying sequins of couture quality. This sketch shows a fireworks gown dubbed "Julie" (production or event unknown). *Collection of Bill Sarrís.*

Chapter Four

Travilla and Monroe

There have been many great partnerships between costume designer and movie star. Just think Adrian and Greta Garbo; Jean Louis and Rita Hayworth; Givenchy and Audrey Hepburn. But there have been none so great as Travilla and Marilyn Monroe, because theirs was also a love story.

Travilla, adjusting one of the many glamorous gowns he designed for Monroe's role as Lorelei in *Gentlemen Prefer Blondes* (1953). *Collection of Bill Sarris.*

"I worked with Marilyn on eight of her movies and I got to know her extremely well. But I also fell in love with her," Travilla said. "It was impossible for any man to be around Marilyn without being aware of her sexuality and without falling for her."

They met in 1950 when Monroe was a newly-signed starlet at Twentieth Century Fox. "I'll never forget our first meeting because it was extraordinary by any standards," Travilla recalled. "I was one of several designers and I had an office that was only about 15 feet wide and 20 feet long, divided in two by a sliding door. At one end was my desk and a couch; beyond the door was a bank of mirrors that served as my fitting room.

"One day this stunning, gorgeous girl walked into my office and said, 'Mr. Travilla, I need to try one some clothes for a photo session. Can I possibly use your fitting room, as it's the only one free?'

"Of course, I said it was OK. She took some bathing suits into the fitting room and closed the door behind her. Minutes later the door slid back and there was this wonderful girl, looking dynamite in a black swimsuit and high heel shoes. She asked my approval, 'What do you think of this one?' She looked great, and I told her so.

"Then suddenly the shoulder strap that held up one side of her swimsuit snapped, and her left breast popped out. That was my introduction to Marilyn Monroe." From that point on, the pair quickly became friends and then lovers.

"We dated for a brief period and if the famous baseball player Joe DiMaggio had not come into Marilyn's life, then I would have pursued our affair further," he said. "But Marilyn had just met Joe. Our period of dating occurred when my wife was away and Joe had gone on the road for a couple of weeks."

The First Date

"The way was left wide open for romance," Travilla continued. "Our first date was like an excerpt from a movie."

He described how, upon going to Monroe's hotel to pick her up, he was kept waiting outside her door for a few minutes. "While I was standing there waiting, a handsome young contract actor, all smartly dressed, also arrived and knocked on Marilyn's door. He was also told to wait."

At this point, both suitors could hear Monroe's voice from inside the room saying, "Just a moment please." In the background was the sound of rustling papers. Then a bellboy arrived with a huge bouquet of flowers for Monroe, and he was told to wait.

"Marilyn had no sense of time," Travilla laughed. "So it didn't matter if she knew you were waiting or not. It was several minutes more before she finally opened the door. She took the flowers; then she looked at the actor standing next to me, and seemed a bit surprised to see him."

The actor reminded Monroe that they had a date but she turned him down: "No, you must have misunderstood. I have a date with Mr. Travilla." After he left and Travilla was finally admitted to her room, he noticed that she had stuffed papers under the bed and chairs in an effort to tidy up. "That was the rustling sound we'd heard!"

But Monroe still wasn't ready. Now it was a matter of which shoes to wear, either a pair of red high heels or flats. "Marilyn was about five feet five and a half, and if she put on the heels she was definitely going to be taller than my five feet eight," Travilla said. "I wasn't bothered by her height, I was just thrilled we had a date!" She spent the next forty-five minutes trying on shoes, until she chose the heels. Then, when they arrived at the nightclub, she kicked them off danced in her stocking feet.

"I probably felt the most good-looking of my life because she looked only at me that night," Travilla recalled. "She never looked to the side and was never aware of the rest of the world, just the guy she was with. She had worried about making me look smaller than her but she made me feel six feet four."

"One night I took Marilyn to see the great blues singer Billie Holiday at the Tiffany Club, which was on 8th street in the middle of Los Angeles. We managed to get ourselves a nice table; then I excused myself to go down the hall to the men's room.

Opposite page: A nightclub snapshot of Marilyn and her Billy, souvenir of their brief love affair. *Collection of Bill Sarris.*

"As I walked, I passed by the manager's office. The door was ajar and I couldn't help but notice that hanging on the wall was Marilyn's famous nude calendar. When I got back at the table I told Marilyn, 'Honey, your calendar's on the wall.' She was like a little excited kid. 'Really? You know, I've never seen it. Let's go and have a look.'

"So we went back and this time the door to the manager's office was closed. What we didn't realize at the time was that Billie was using it as a dressing room. Anyway, Marilyn knocked on the door and a tall black man answered it and said, 'Yes, what can we do for you?' Now, I figured Billie had heard Marilyn was in the audience, so in answer to the question I said all we wanted to do was see the calendar on the wall.

"Suddenly, from where we were standing in the hallway, we saw the arm of Billie Holiday—we never saw her face—reach up and grab the calendar. She crumpled it and then threw it in Marilyn's face. We heard her saying, 'Here you are, b——.'

"We couldn't believe what had happened, and of course we were terribly offended. I told the manager we were leaving. He begged us to stay, and promised us the best table in the room, but we left in disgust. That might have been the end of the matter, except a journalist picked up on the story.

"He quoted the owner of the Tiffany Club saying that as I was dating Marilyn Monroe, I was offended at seeing her nude photo on the wall, and got in a fist fight over it. Which of course was all a lie, but that's how the paper wrote it. So that's what my wife Dona read when she arrived back in town, ready to kill me!"

True Friends

Their affair was short-lived, given that Travilla was still married and Monroe was about to become engaged to Joe DiMaggio. But he would remain one of her few true friends and confidantes. It was as if he could see the inner Monroe, who he called "a combination of a five-year-old child with gold curly locks and an incredibly sensual woman."

When Monroe married DiMaggio in January 1954, Travilla slipped easily into a new role of friendship. His first gesture was to add a white mink collar and rhinestone buttons to a plain suit she had purchased off-the-rack, making it prettier for her civil service wedding.

Monroe on her wedding day, in the suit modified by Travilla. *United Press International.*

More meaningfully, he was there when she needed someone to talk to. "Sometimes Marilyn would call me up when she was depressed," he said. "It was usually late at night, and it was very annoying for my wife to pick up the phone after we'd both gone to bed, only to hear that cute little voice on the end of the line."

He would accept the call, trying to "talk her around" on the phone. When that didn't work, he would go to her in person. "It made my wife even more unhappy, but off I'd go to Marilyn and I'd find her perhaps despondent, and talking of killing herself."

Travilla would stay with her for hours. "To cheer her up I would laugh and talk and clown, and wait until she was in a happy mood, so I would feel it safe to leave her and go home in the knowledge that she would live through the night."

For her part, Monroe would express her fears. "She talked about her mother and grandmother and how they had lost their mental ability and died in sanitariums. She told me with fear in her voice, 'It's going to happen to me.'"

Despite this recurring scenario, Travilla was one of those who refused to believe that Monroe committed suicide in August 1962. "I know people think that she took her own life," he said. "But I know very well that she didn't."

To his way of thinking, "Marilyn could never have gone out by her own hand the *way* she did. She would have made a show of it. She would have had full makeup, satin bedsheets . . . maybe she would have been wearing a beautiful negligee." Travilla imagined that she would have worn the one he designed for her, a star-quality gown with ostrich plumes. "Then she would have taken a sleeping pill and been found looking beautiful."

It is touching that Travilla persisted in this romantic image of Monroe's last moments, despite the fact that he knew she did *not* always strive to look beautiful. Earlier in their relationship, Travilla had been chagrined by her habit of putting lanolin on her face and hair "until she looked messy and greasy." It was as if she dressed to be noticed, one way or another.

As Travilla once said, with reference to the speculation that she had multiple personalities: "There were only two Marilyn Monroes that people ever saw. One was fully painted and gloriously beautiful; the other was disheveled and greasy, and often not looking too clean."

An Act of Love

Over the years, Travilla often advised Monroe on what to wear, and presumably helped to cultivate what he called her "gloriously beautiful" image. He designed her movie costumes, of course, but he also created gowns for her publicity events and personal appearances.

"My clothes for Marilyn were an act of love," he said. "Because I adored her, I couldn't help but do my best for her." Indeed, the only famous gown he did not design for her was the sequined soufflé clinger that she wore while singing "Happy Birthday" to John F. Kennedy at Madison Square Garden on May 19, 1962. It was designed by Jean Louis, because it was at a time when Travilla was out of town.

"Designing for Marilyn was a joy because she was so beautiful, and because she needed me," Travilla once commented. "She needed the protection of what I could do for her.

"I loved to have my clothes make her look even more beautiful. And I never had to do more than one sketch for her outfits, because we thought so closely," Travilla said. "She was the most complex, incredible, magnificent woman. She was the love of my life, that girl."

Opposite page: This ruched, bias-cut evening gown was designed by Travilla for one of Monroe's personal appearances. *Collection of Bill Sarris.*

Chapter Five

The Monroe Movies

With regard to costuming Monroe, Travilla's main problem was finding enough changes for the numerous publicity shots Twentieth Century Fox had to churn out in order to keep up with the demand from the fan magazines.

"It didn't matter if they had just run Marilyn on the cover, they'd agree to interview some other actress only if the studio provided yet another photo of Marilyn," he recalled.

"She wouldn't go to a gallery sitting without me. The studio would have to bring me in for the day, and I'd take a piece of biased satin, wrap it over her naked body, and they would shoot her. There were no more clothes left in wardrobe to put on her, for all the photographs needed by the world! Otherwise, all I had to worry about were the censors."

Travilla was speaking of the early 1950s, when the Motion Picture Association headed by Joseph Breen could censor almost any aspect of a Hollywood movie, based on the industry's self-imposed Production Code.

"Belly buttons were out and so was showing the inside of a thigh," he explained. "As for breasts, nothing could be revealed, not even a shadow. If I cut a V-neckline, the breasts had to be totally inside the garment. That was relatively easy with Marilyn, since her breasts were perfectly pointed outward!"

Travilla designed Monroe's costumes for eight of her most memorable movies, seven of which are profiled here. [Unfortunately, none of his original sketches are extant for *Don't Bother to Knock* (1952).] These movies were all produced by Twentieth Century Fox in the prolific years 1952 to 1956, during Travilla's tenure as a contract designer for the studio.

This vintage postcard shows Monroe's "perfect breasts" displayed to advantage in her songstress costume for *Bus Stop* (1956). *Collection of Bill Sarris.*

Opposite page: An Italian fan magazine featured Monroe in one of Travilla's costumes for *Gentlemen Prefer Blondes. Collection of Bill Sarris.*

Monkey Business (1952)

As the ditzy secretary of absent-minded professor Cary Grant, Monroe is a love interest foil for Grant's wife Ginger Rogers, in this screwball comedy about the youth-inducing effects of an experimental formula.

Travilla acknowledged that "the only costume of mine that Marilyn ever hated" was the one he made for her roller-skating sequence in *Monkey Business*. "She was not yet a movie star . . . and she had yet to do a film where the public would sit up and say, 'this is the girl!' So every costume was important to her, and she only had three changes in this movie."

The director, Howard Hawks, insisted on a full skirt for this scene. "I made her a very attractive, tan-colored jersey wool dress with a pleated skirt cut from two full circles of cloth. There was no petticoat but it looked pretty." Still, it hid her figure, and Monroe refused to wear it. The director prevailed, at which point she tried to skate with the pleats tucked between her legs, in a scene cut from the movie.

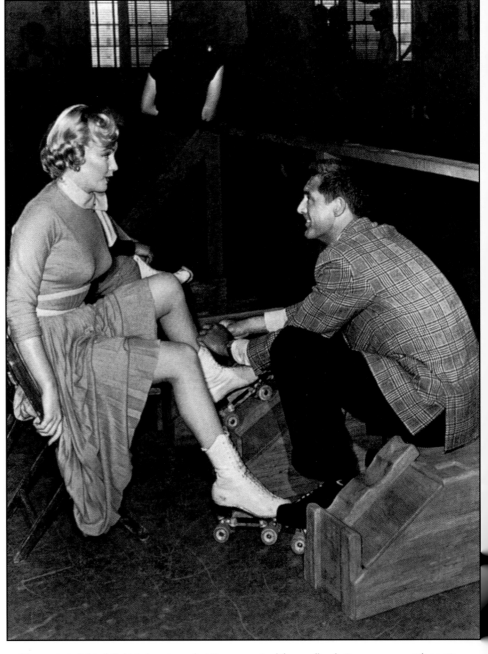

Monroe hated this full-skirted costume, but it was required for a roller-skating sequence with co-star Cary Grant. *Collection of Bill Sarris.*

Travilla used pom-poms to emphasize Monroe's comic role. *Collection of Bill Sarris.*

Ginger Rogers is ready to dance in this test shot for *Monkey Business*. She was billed above Monroe, and her wardrobe was much more extensive. *Collection of Bill Sarris.*

Two American chorus girls head for the fertile gold-digging grounds of Paris in this comic exploit based on the roguish novel written by Anita Loos in 1925. The movie features many dance numbers with Jane Russell (Dorothy) and Marilyn Monroe (Lorelei), and both gals get married to their men in the end.

Burlesque had long been a specialty for Travilla and he excelled in this movie, which was a real showcase for fishnet, frills, and feathers. But the most famous costume, the hot pink gown he designed for the "Diamonds are a Girl's Best Friend" dance routine, was almost conservative. It was also one of the fastest designs he'd ever executed, done on an emergency basis to overcome objections by the censors.

"That gown was something I came up with after the studio rejected my first costume—which Marilyn loved," Travilla said. The first one was extremely revealing and it was quickly canned when it came out that Monroe had done some nude photography during an earlier stage of her career.

"There were problems with the censors all during filming," Travilla ruefully recalled. "When it came out about the nude photos, that was about it."

87

Marilyn Monroe
and
Jane Russell

Travilla

Travilla drew a
composite portrait for
this sketch since both
actresses would be
wearing the rose-
bodice costume.
Collection of Bill Sarris.

The production records for *Gentlemen Prefer Blondes* show that the Motion Picture Association sent numerous censorship letters to Colonel Jason Joy of Fox, cutting lines and rejecting costumes.

In a missive from November 1952 the Association warned: "The business of the girls dressing should be kept within the careful limits of good taste. We have already rejected one costume suggested for this scene."

According to a file memo of March 1953, the Association informed the studio by telephone that the diamond-studded costumes "were unacceptable by reason of being overly sex suggestive."

Monroe, posing front and back in the original "Diamonds" costume. Each stone was hand-positioned and welded onto the underlying bodystocking. Travilla was justly proud of the work he'd put into creating the original showgirl costume, and he later re-styled it for Betty Grable to wear when she opened her nightclub act in Las Vegas. *Collection of Greg Schreiner.*

The New "Diamonds" Costume

"The first costume . . . made it appear that her body was covered by nothing more than a pair of fishnet hose that traveled up her torso to just under her breasts. Then a harness of rhinestones traveled around her hips and fell into a ponytail at her back, with black Bird of Paradise feathers. Marilyn had to stand for hours while the jeweler and I shaped everything to her body, then we soldered the jewels on. We were very strategic, there was even a jewel in front of each nipple!"

Travilla was given two days to come up with a new design that would not be too revealing. One that would, in fact, cover her up. "I took a brilliant candy-pink silk *peau d'ange* and flattened that to green billiard felt. Apart from two side seams, the dress was folded into shape, rather like cardboard. Any other girl would have looked like she was *wearing* cardboard, but on the screen I swear you would have thought Marilyn had on a pale, thin piece of silk. Her body was so fabulous it still came through!"

Travilla explained how he "crunched the whole thing in, with a belt at the waist and a huge bow at the back. For oomph, we added full-length gloves in a matching pink, and loaded her arms with diamond bracelets."

That was it, a film icon was born. Later, after Travilla started his own private-label clothing business, he preferred the mystique of a high neckline and was quoted as saying: "It's an old rule that mystery, not diamonds, are a girl's best friend."

The hot pink dress for "Diamonds Are a Girl's Best Friend," designed as a last-minute substitute for a diamond-studded showgirl costume. *Collection of Bill Sarris.*

Opposite page: Travilla and a sketch of the revised "Diamonds" gown, with sketches of the first design in the background. *Collection of Bill Sarris.*

Another costume check for *Gentlemen Prefer Blondes*. This showgirl look was worn by both Monroe and co-star Jane Russell. The heavy red crepe sparkles with sequins, the slit skirt adds pizzazz. *Collection of George P. Erengis.*

More costume tests for the stateroom interior and
the wedding scene in *Gentlemen Prefer Blondes*.
Collection of Greg Schreiner.

How to Marry a Millionaire (1953)

Three models played by Marilyn Monroe, Betty Grable, and Lauren Bacall set their sights on snagging millionaire husbands. After many mishaps, they each marry their dream mate, one of whom actually is a millionaire. They all dress to play the part of high society, with a fashion sequence thrown in for good measure.

An asymmetric halter was sexy without revealing cleavage. This satin and sequin gown was in a fantasy sequence featuring multiple mirrors. *Collection of Bill Sarris.*

LADIES - WARDROBE

PICT. DATE

TITLE 705 A

DIRECTOR NEGULESCO

ACTOR Marilyn Monroe

CHARACTER Pola

CHANGE 5-A
DRESSING-ROOM

SET INT. SALON

SCENE G-39-TehG3.
DES TRAVILLA
COLOR 8X10

A costume check of Monroe's beach outfit, which was used in the
movie's fashion sequence. *Collection of Greg Schreiner.*

This still of the fashion sequence shows the red bathing suit that became one of Monroe's most photographed looks. The diversity of these costumes, all designed by Travilla, showcase his talents. *Academy of Motion Picture Arts and Sciences.*

Given the censorship run-in during the production of *Gentlemen Prefer Blondes*, Travilla was extremely careful in this movie. For a gown to be worn by Monroe in one scene, which was eventually all but cut from the last sequence, he was taxed to create the look of deep cleavage without even the shadow of a breast showing.

In typical Travilla fashion, he engineered a gold lamé sunburst-pleated dress that would hug her curves—with a plunging neckline that stayed in place thanks to a hidden wire running straight up from her waistline.

The gold lamé dress, one of Monroe's favorite designs, was shown only briefly in the movie. *Collection of Bill Sarris.*

Gold-plated Monroe in a publicity photo.
Collection of Bill Sarris.

This same gown caused a sensation when Monroe insisted on wearing it to a *Photoplay* awards ceremony where she would be named Fastest Rising Star of 1952. Travilla vividly recalled fighting with Monroe over her decision to wear it in public.

"When Marilyn asked me for the dress, I told her she couldn't have it. It's a costume . . . so delicate it wouldn't take a zipper, we had to baste the back seam together by hand."

He wanted to spare her from embarrassment, cautioning: "It's too tight. People will laugh at you." But she went over his head to Daryl Zanuck, who ordered Travilla to give Marilyn whatever she wanted to wear.

Defeated, Travilla still issued a set of rules along with the dress. "I told her to wear very little jewelry, earrings and nothing more, and keep her hair simple. And for God's sake, to walk like a lady." She followed his rules to the letter, but for the last.

The evening went well until Marilyn was called to the stage to accept her award. "To get to the stage, she had to move around the edge of a table, and as she did so her right hip swayed outwards and then back again," Travilla recalled. Suddenly, she was in her hip-swinging walk, to a roar from several male members of the star-studded audience.

"This was not the end of it. Joan Crawford, spotting a chance of publicity for herself, called all the reporters and blasted Marilyn." The gist of Crawford's tirade was that Monroe's skirt was so tight, her rear end resembled two puppies wrestling under the bedcovers. Regardless of such criticism, the fans loved Monroe's sexy swagger. Her star power was not diminished and was perhaps even bolstered by this incident.

MARILYN MONROE
CHANGE 14 - INT. OF SHIPS BALLROOM
MONTAGE 'A'
"GENTLEMEN PREFER BLONDS"

Travilla

Another version of the gold lamé dress that caused such consternation. *Collection of Bill Sarris.*

River of No Return (1954)

Set in the Wild West of 1875, this film pairs Marilyn Monroe with Robert Mitchum. Monroe's character, a saloon singer girl, falls in love with Mitchum, who was once wrongly sent to jail for shooting a man in defense of another. Together with Mitchum's ten-year-old son, the pair make a raft journey on a raging river during which they encounter danger from outlaws and Indians.

In this tribute to Irving Berlin, Ethel Merman and Dan Dailey form a vaudeville act as The Five Donahues with their three offspring played by Donald O'Connor, Mitzi Gaynor, and Johnnie Ray. Enter Marilyn Monroe, the nightclub singer (Vicky) who enchants O'Connor and angers Merman. The grande finale number features the movie's title song, where all are reconciled.

Playing a nightclub singer, Monroe lights up the stage like a firecracker in this spectacular sequined gown. Photo, Academy of Motion Picture Arts and Sciences. Sketch, collection of Bill Sarris.

Marilyn Monroe
"There's no business
like Show business
20th Century Fox

Travilla

Marilyn Monroe
729-28 Dress
Edna
729-29 Headpiece
Lucy

Nightclub singer or not, Monroe could also look classy, as in this cream and wool sheath with a dyed-to-match fox stole. *Collection of Bill Sarris.*

904-65

Mitzi Gaynor in a rhumba costume attributed to Travilla. According to Bill Sarris, Travilla eventually walked off the production due to a contract dispute and another designer was brought in. However, Monroe insisted that only Travilla could design *her* costumes. *Academy of Motion Picture Arts and Sciences.*

Travilla

Great south-of-the-border style for the "Having a Heat Wave" routine. Collection of Bill Sarris.

The action heats up with thigh-high skirting for Monroe, as seen in this publicity still. *Academy of Motion Picture Arts and Sciences.*

Travilla posed with his original costume for "Heat Wave" at a 1990 costume exhibit in Orange County, California. *Academy of Motion Picture Arts and Sciences.*

This cross-tied halter top showed more cleavage than most of Travilla's designs for Monroe. She wore it for a party scene in *The Seven Year Itch* (see opposite page). *Collection of Bill Sarris.*

The Seven Year Itch (1955)

Tom Ewell reprises his Broadway role as a husband whose wife goes on a brief vacation with their children. He remains behind in New York on business, alone for the first time in seven years of marriage, and begins fantasizing about a model who has sublet the apartment above. Marilyn Monroe plays The Girl with her characteristic mix of innocence and sexual allure.

The Seven Year Itch storyline, unlike some of Monroe's earlier films, held forth no promise as a costume showcase. It was not a period piece and she had no dance routines. Still, this was to become the vehicle for Travilla's most famous dress design, in bias-cut crepe with a halter top and sunburst pleats.

It was a deceptively simple dress, classic but sexy, and it was meant to make Monroe look cool on the hot, sticky sidewalks of New York. "I'm going to have my precious baby standing over a grate," Travilla remembered. "I wanted her to look fresh and clean.

"So I wondered what could I do with this most beautiful girl that Marilyn was to play to make her look clean, talcum-powdered, and adorable," Travilla mused. "What would I give her to wear that would blow in the breeze and be fun and pretty? I knew there would be a wind blowing so that would require a skirt."

Body-conscious as always, Marilyn refused to wear panties for the fittings, causing one studio seamstress to refuse to pin her. Another fitter was called in, but Marilyn didn't put on underpants until the day she had to wear them for the camera.

When she stood over the subway grate and a blast of air caused her pleated skirt to swirl above her waist, Monroe made Hollywood history. Travilla's contribution was all but forgotten, although he often mused in private about the fame of The Dress.

"Here's how famous it was," he said. "We were traveling in London to promote the Littlewoods catalog in the 1970s, and my copy of the dress was on display along with millions of dollars in jewelry." There was a break-in at the show, but the only item stolen was The Dress (which was later anonymously returned).

Fame may be fleeting, but worldwide recognition for that pleated skirt once prompted Travilla to wisecrack: "When I die, don't have me cremated, have me pleated."

Incidentally, one of Travilla's other designs for Monroe—the white terrycloth bathrobe that she dons after a bathtub scene—also rose to icon status. Like the dress, the robe made Monroe look sexy and innocent at the same time, playing on her elusive allure as a child-woman.

*Marilyn Monroe
"7 Year Itch"
Wind scene at Subway*

Travilla

Marilyn Monroe told Travilla that she loved this dress. Neither of them could guess how famous it was to become, as shot at 2:00 a.m. on November 9, 1954, outside the Trans-Luxe Theatre in New York. *Collection of Bill Sarris.*

Bus Stop (1956)

A young and naïve cowboy played by Don Murray falls for the café singer played by Marilyn Monroe during a rodeo event in Phoenix. She flees after he makes a premature marriage proposal, but he finds her and forces her onto a bus that will take them back to his hometown in Montana. They work out their differences during a protracted bus stop.

Travilla used "two-dollar rayon" to make a suitably cheap black skirt, for the rodeo scene in *Bus Stop*. Interestingly, the lacy peasant blouse used in this scene had been worn earlier by Susan Hayward, for *With A Song In My Heart* (1952). *Academy of Motion Picture Arts and Sciences.*

Chapter Six

A Movie Sampler

A handful of the movies that Travilla worked on were documented by his costume sketches, memorabilia, and notes. These are presented here, to the extent that original material was available.

Ann Sheridan posed in a smart suit for day and a glamorous negligee for night, in these publicity stills attributed to *Nora Prentiss* (1947). *Collection of Bill Sarris.*

Nora Prentiss (1947)

Ann Sheridan plays nightclub singer Nora Prentiss, who meets a rather reserved doctor after a minor accident. He is smitten and convinces her to begin an affair, even though he is married. Soon he is faced with divorce or the loss of Nora. Then, in typical film noir style, a patient dies in his office, leaving another option.

My Wild Irish Rose (1947)

This is a sentimental romp in vaudeville of the 1880s, centered on the life story of Irish tenor Chauncey Olcott, who is played by Dennis Morgan. In real life, Olcott wrote the title song; in the movie, he sings it for his true love Rose, played by Arlene Dahl.

A duo of sketches for *My Wild Irish Rose*, set in the late nineteenth century. *Collection of Bill Sarris.*

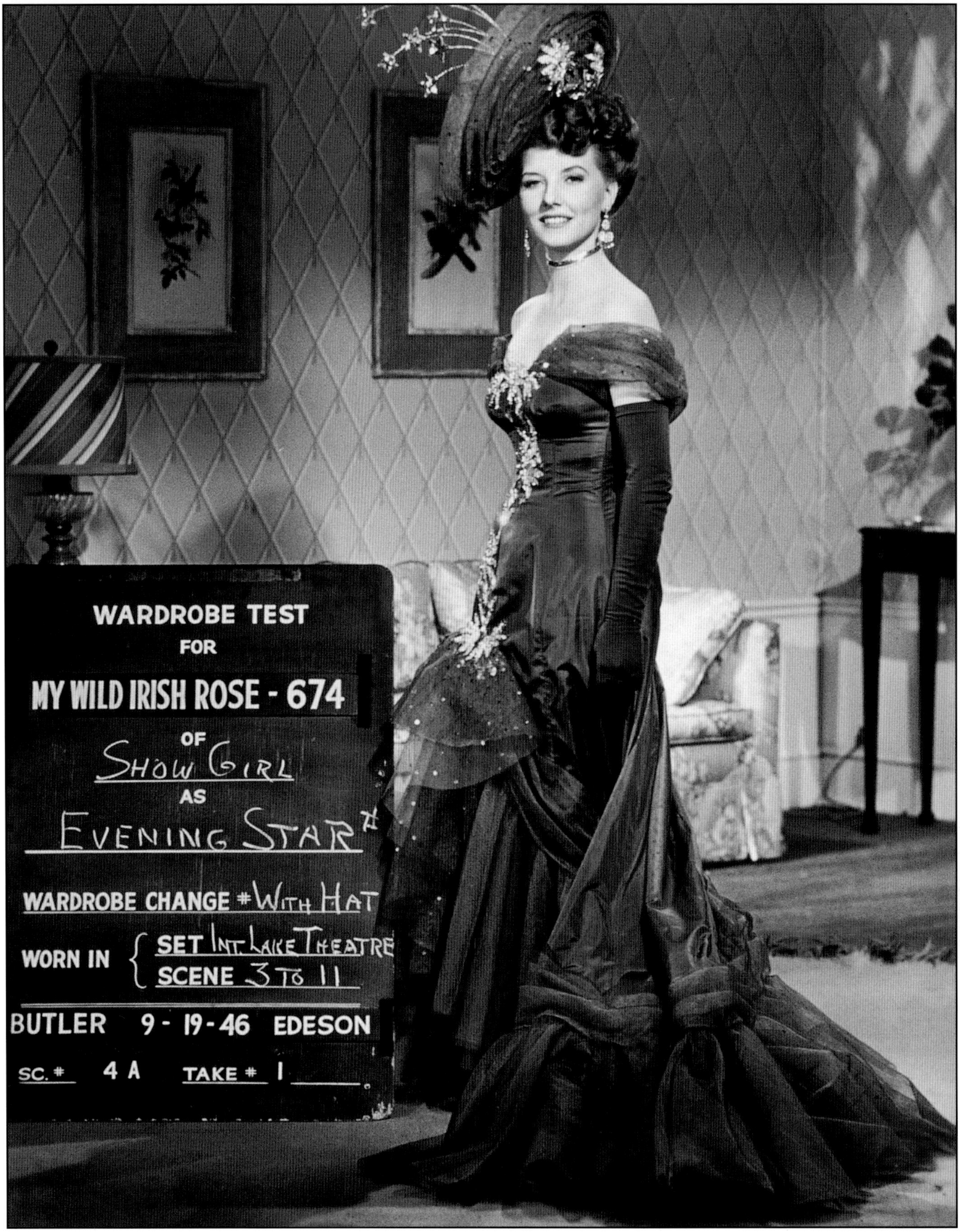
WARDROBE TEST
FOR
MY WILD IRISH ROSE - 674
OF
SHOW GIRL
AS
EVENING STAR
WARDROBE CHANGE # WITH HAT
WORN IN
SET INT. LAKE THEATRE
SCENE 3 TO 11
BUTLER 9-19-46 EDESON
SC. # 4 A TAKE # 1

Checking the "Evening Star" showgirl costume. *Collection of Bill Sarris.*

Travilla with Arlene Dahl on the set of *Wild Irish*.
Collection of *Bill Sarris*.

115

The Adventures of Don Juan (1949)

Loosely based on the legendary escapades of a romantic nobleman in Spain, shortly after the defeat of the Spanish Armada. This movie features Erroll Flynn at his swashbuckling best. He seduces many women, including a lady-in-waiting played by Viveca Lindfors, but always with good heart. He also manages to save the monarchy from being overthrown.

When Travilla was still a neophyte designer at Twentieth Century Fox, he was selected by box office magnet Erroll Flynn to remake his costumes for a big-budget costume epic, *The Adventures of Don Juan*. The studio had originally assigned another designer with more seniority, Marjorie Best.

"The reason I got the job is typical Errol Flynn," Travilla recalled. Apparently, Best had a fine reputation for costume epics and had carefully researched late sixteenth century Spain. The result was too accurate for Flynn, given the flounces and lace, jeweled garters, and powdered wigs that were emblematic of masculine dress in that era.

"Bearing in mind his image as the great lover, Errol took one look at these clothes that had been made for a small fortune, and declared he would not wear them! He thought he'd look like a poof and be a laughing stock, and I think he was right.

"Errol was mindful of my work on *Silver River*, and he said to Jack Warner: "If anyone can make Ann Sheridan look good, they can sure dress me!" So that's how I got the job. What's more, it wasn't Travilla's first assignment with Flynn. A decade earlier, he had costumed him in silk, velvet, and hip boots for the Warner Brothers' historical epic *Elizabeth and Essex* (1939).

By the time he began shooting *Don Juan*, Flynn was thirty-eight years old and starting to show signs of the wild lifestyle that had made him such a legendary figure. "He was a real lady's man and not just on screen, but off as well. He'd had many years of womanizing, hard drinking, smoking some 100 cigarettes a day, and (as I later found out) dabbling with opium.

"It all took its toll, but I had to make him look like the sexiest guy who ever lived and I certainly wasn't going to do that with bloomers and ruffles.

"I had to change the period just enough to dress him in a virile way. I cut his jackets down to the waist and gave him open-neck shirts to show off his chest. I belted his waist and put a dagger at his side, then put him in tights and boots. Errol loved the look, and my career really took off at Fox from then on."

Travilla won an Oscar for costuming Flynn in *The Adventures of Don Juan*, along with the rest of the design team. (Costumes for the other leads and ensemble were by Marjorie Best and Leah Rhodes.)

Flynn reclining in Viveca Lindfors's lap (her gown was by Leah Rhodes). *Collection of Bill Sarris.*

Errol Flynn struts his swashbuckling stuff in these test shots. *Collection of Bill Sarris.*

Flamingo Road (1949)

In this fine example of film noir, Joan Crawford plays a carnival dancer who tries to make a normal life for herself in a small Southern town. She falls in love with a local boy whose political aspirations cause him to reject her for a debutante. She vows to make it big someday, and does so by marrying a politico from the opposite party. They move to a mansion on the town's Flamingo Road, but she's haunted by her past love until she confronts the political boss who caused their unhappiness.

Travilla often alluded to the fact that his assignments were never difficult, just challenging. His life, however, could be made miserable by the temperament of the leads he had to dress for a given movie. "Some people, no matter how hard you try, just can't be satisfied," he said. "I found that true with Joan Crawford, when Fox assigned me to her for *Flamingo Road*.

"Joan was playing a poor carnival dancer, and her first test shots were in close-up only. So I loaned her a sweater, just something I had in stock that I thought might work for that sequence. I also loaned her a skirt, it wouldn't even show in the tests."

Testing the testy Crawford in costumes designed for her poor-girl beginnings. *Collection of Bill Sarris.*

"Flamingo Road"
#12.

sc 162 – 173
3rd Cafe
Joan Crawford
as
"Lane

Crawford in a
black cocktailer
with dagger-point
darts, for a
nightclub scene
after she's made it
in high society.
*Collection of Bill
Sarris.*

"I was fitting another actress the next day, when I got a call from the assistant director asking me to come to the set: 'Miss Crawford does not like the skirt.' I said I couldn't come, and carried on with the fitting. Joan went into a fury! She walked briskly all the way from the set on Stage 22 to my office, and by the time she got there she was seething. She slammed the door open so hard, the knob went clean through the wall and stuck fast.

"Then she exploded! Joan took no account of the fact that another actress was there, and her tirade included more four-letter words than I'd ever heard from a woman before. Later that day, a beautiful bouquet of flowers arrived for me, with a sincere note of apology.

"Joan was also a tyrant to fit. She made her mark in clothes by MGM's ace designer Adrian, with a special look that she wasn't ready to give up. I had so many problems with her on *Flamingo Road* that, while I was happy to loan her my patterns, I wouldn't make or fit the clothes myself."

But Crawford's legendary temper was just one aspect of her personality, as Travilla later acknowledged. "After I'd left the studio and ventured on my own, Joan proved what a lady she could really be. I was showing a collection at the Plaza Hotel in New York, and Joan came to see my clothes. She was a vision in brilliant green, with a silk print dress and matching turban. Even her gloves, bag and shoes were dyed the same shade of emerald," he said.

"My models were showing her the collection, when the head buyers of a store that was very important to me arrived. They joined us, and of course they were thrilled to meet the great Joan Crawford!

"When the repeat showing began, she got up to leave. Putting on her green silk coat, which was lined in the same print as her dress, Joan shook hands all around and said: 'I'll give you a call about the clothes I want, Billy. I took down all the numbers.' I'll never forget it; that was a lovely thing for her to say in front of the buyers."

David and Bathsheba (1951)

Gregory Peck brought humanity to King David, whose lust for a general's wife all but destroyed his kingdom in Old Testament days. He is first captivated by the beautiful Bathsheba, played by Susan Hayward, when he sees her emerging from her bath.

A publicity still of Bathsheba as *odalisque*, played by a languid Susan Hayward. *Academy of Motion Picture Arts and Sciences.*

David and Bathsheba featured exotic dancing in the "India Song" by none other than Gwyn Verdon. She was suitably costumed in gold and silk. Note the changes from the sketch on this page to the camera test on the opposite page. *Collection of Bill Sarris.*

GWEN VERDON
DANCE SEQUENCE
"DAVID & BATHSHEBA"

Travilla

123

Half Angel (1951)

Playing a sincere nurse one minute and a sleep-walking vamp the next, Loretta Young manages to be wooed by a bemused Joseph Cotton. Young's wardrobe reflected her dual-natured personality with prim and proper attire for her true self and a languid, sexy wardrobe for her alter ego.

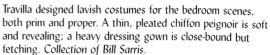

Travilla designed lavish costumes for the bedroom scenes, both prim and proper. A thin, pleated chiffon peignoir is soft and revealing; a heavy dressing gown is close-bound but fetching. *Collection of Bill Sarris.*

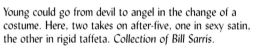

Young could go from devil to angel in the change of a costume. Here, two takes on after-five, one in sexy satin, the other in rigid taffeta. *Collection of Bill Sarris.*

Viva Zapata! (1951)

The story of Mexican revolutionary Emiliano Zapata, as played by Marlon Brando with Jean Peters as his romantic lead. Also starring Anthony Quinn as his brother and fellow soldier.

Viva Zapata! called for peasant costumes, the same as for *Cabo Blanco*, but this time Travilla felt challenged. In fact, although justifiably proud of his Oscar for *The Adventures of Don Juan*, Travilla felt he should have at least been nominated for *Zapata!*

"I created the clothes and then I rubbed them with a rock, rolled them on the ground, and oil-stained them. Then I washed them and oil-stained them some more, abused them and ripped them to age them. No one knew what I had done because the clothes just fitted in, blended in."

Travilla found Marlon Brando "marvelous to work with" but was "most pleased" with the work he did for leading lady Jean Peters. "I figured she would be from an upper Mexican family in a small village so I decided to dress her five years out-of-date (it would have taken that long for fashions to reach where she lived).

"My big problem with Jean was that she was beautifully formed in an American kind of body; that is, long-waisted and tall, with a great healthy stride in her walk." Travilla solved this problem by creating a padded form to be worn by Peters under her garments to create "a Mexican body with higher hips."

His next challenge was getting rid of her American walk. "That's when I hit upon the idea of asking Jean if I could change her shoe size. She agreed and I made her half-button shoes a half-size too small, and uncomfortable. She immediately lost that American walk and became the little lady of the village."

Camera checks for Jean Peters as a padded peasant in *Viva Zapata!* Collection of Bill Sarris.

126

Gentlemen Marry Brunettes (1955)

A *frothy* sequel to Gentlemen Prefer Blondes. *Featuring Jane Russell, Gentlemen Marry Brunettes was released by her own independent production company.*

It's the French touch for Russell, poodle and all. *Collection of Bill Sarris.*

127

One of the many
glamorous gowns
designed for
Brunettes.
Collection of Bill
Sarris.

128

An elegant gray after-five dress for Russell's arrival in Monte Carlo. *Collection of Bill Sarris.*

Another showgirl showstopper, showcasing Russell's voluptuous figure. *Academy of Motion Picture Arts and Sciences.*

129

"I had always loved Jane ever since I had once come into her dressing room as she was looking at herself in the mirror," Travilla recalled. "That's when she said, self-mockingly: 'Goddamn, you're so beautiful. If only you could act!'"

Red fringe creates a saucy, sexy look for Russell in the role of Mimi. *Collection of Bill Sarris.*

From The Terrace (1960)

In this film, based on a novel by John O'Hara, Paul Newman plays a young man who has a hard time adjusting to civilian life after his tour in the Army. When he marries a chic blue-blood played by Joanne Woodward, they begin a life of bitterness.

Travilla convinced Joanne Woodward to "think tall" and experiment with a new silhouette for this film, which required her to wear "tons of beautiful clothes." The series of costume checks shown here gives some idea as to the extent of Woodward's wardrobe.

For two outdoors shots, Travilla styled Woodward crisp, clear colors. *Collection of Bill Sarris.*

The scene card read "interior of Alfred's New York apartment." It must have been a ritzy address given these elegant looks. *Collection of Bill Sarris.*

Part of: Mary

Change # 15   Hair # 7
Scene 113

WORN   Int. Alfreds Apt - NY

Part of: Mary
Change # 13   Hair # 4.
Worn: Scs 92
        Int Alfred's N.Y. Apt.
DARKER MOUTH   MORE EYE MAKE UP

Woodward looks regal, in spectacular satin evening gowns. *Collection of Bill Sarris.*

A sparkling black ballgown, with and without its matching stole. *Collection of Bill Sarris.*

For an elegant hostess gown, Travilla cut ombre gold brocade simply, then wrapped and tied it with a strategic leg slit. *Collection of Bill Sarris*.

Joanne Woodward
8
THE STRIPPER

Travilla

A daytime look cut from clingy silk, for when Woodward wasn't stripping. *Collection of Bill Sarris.*

The Stripper (1963)

A moral tale in which Joanne Woodward stepped out of her ladylike image—and her clothes—to portray a professional striptease dancer.

"Once I had been assigned to the film, I started to assess the character of the stripper. I figured firstly that she had to be a night person, someone who works at night and sleeps late into the day," Travilla said. "I decided she was someone who was very aware of herself, who probably lay out naked under the sun and was deeply tanned, and wore a lot of white."

With this image in mind, Travilla decided to dress Joanne Woodward in silk and other sheer fabrics that would reveal the movement of her body, for her off-work wardrobe. "But here was a problem because Joanne's breasts were small." His solution was to create breast cards that would glue onto her body and move naturally.

"So I called in the [studio] sculptor to make some plaster casts of Joanne's body. From these casts they made another form just as Joanne was, and then they made breasts of clay that fitted on top, until they met my approval," he said. "What I wanted to see was . . . nothing too much, just beautiful breasts that scoop up and move."

To complete the process, the sculptor formed a mold from the modeling clay, and then cast the pads in tissue-thin foam that could be glued directly onto Woodward's body. The pads even had air vents, and could be worn without a bra. But they were so delicate, they would tear upon removal and had to be replaced for each day of shooting. "It was a tribute to Joanne as an actress that she went through all this for the role."

Valley of the Dolls (1967)

An exposé of the drugs, desperation, and destruction behind Hollywood film making based on Jacqueline Susann's bestselling book of the same name. Starring Patty Duke, Susan Hayward, Barbara Parkins, and Sharon Tate.

This is one production in which Travilla was offered an acting role, as the costume designer husband of Patty Duke's movie star character. It called for a scene in which she returned home from the studio, only to find him swimming naked in their pool with a starlet. The script called for the swimmers to run off into the bushes, still nude.

The producer assured Travilla that the camera would only show him from the rear, but he still wasn't convinced about the propriety of a nude role. "I have customers out there who pay many hundreds of dollars [for my clothing designs] . . . and they won't appreciate seeing my bare ass running across the screen!"

Jennifer

8

Ext Music Center   151 – 134
Int Tony's Home   155 – 15

Travilla

A decade after *Valley of the Dolls*, Travilla was praised for his design of such "timeless" clothing. This evening look in silver and copper Lurex cloth is a good example. *Collection of Bill Sarris.*

138

Another costume originally intended for Garland, worn by her replacement Susan Hayward. The pantsuit is richly beaded over autumnal shades of brocade. *Collection of Bill Sarris.*

Ironically, in its final version only the girlfriend was seen fleeing the pool, so Travilla passed up a chance at stardom for naught. Perhaps it's just as well, since many film historians believe *Valley of the Dolls* was jinxed. Consider the tragic deaths of two leading ladies: Sharon Tate, who was gruesomely murdered by Charles Manson; and Judy Garland, who died of a drug overdose widely believed to have been suicide.

Tate played a fragile beauty whose love (and life) are doomed. During filming, she struck Travilla as "one of the most beautiful, sweetest and nicest actresses I had the pleasure of working with and getting to know." In sharp contrast, he saw Judy Garland as a tragic figure—fragile and nervous. He observed how Garland was literally wasting away.

"In fittings, I became aware of the skin on Judy's body. It was as if there was no life left in her skin; her body was dissipated." She was drinking on the set; finally, her behavior became so erratic that she was fired in mid-production. Travilla was one of the first people Garland called, when she heard rumors that she was about to be fired.

"I went along with her . . . that I couldn't believe they had fired her . . . [and said] the way to find out was to hear it from the producer. Then I called up the producer straight away and told him to expect Judy to phone him. I let him know she was terribly upset and had been crying on the phone to me."

Garland was to have played an aging, tough-as-nails Broadway singer who has weathered it all, including bouts with the bottle. In some ways, the role mirrored Garland's own history with substance abuse.

When she left *Valley of the Dolls*, Garland asked Travilla to give her the clothes he'd made for her role. This he refused to do, since they were studio property, but he made copies of her favorite outfits for her personal wardrobe.

This paisley tunic pant sets was one of Garland's favorite costumes from her aborted role in *Valley of the Dolls*. When she was fired, Travilla copied it for her personal wardrobe. *Collection of Bill Sarris*.

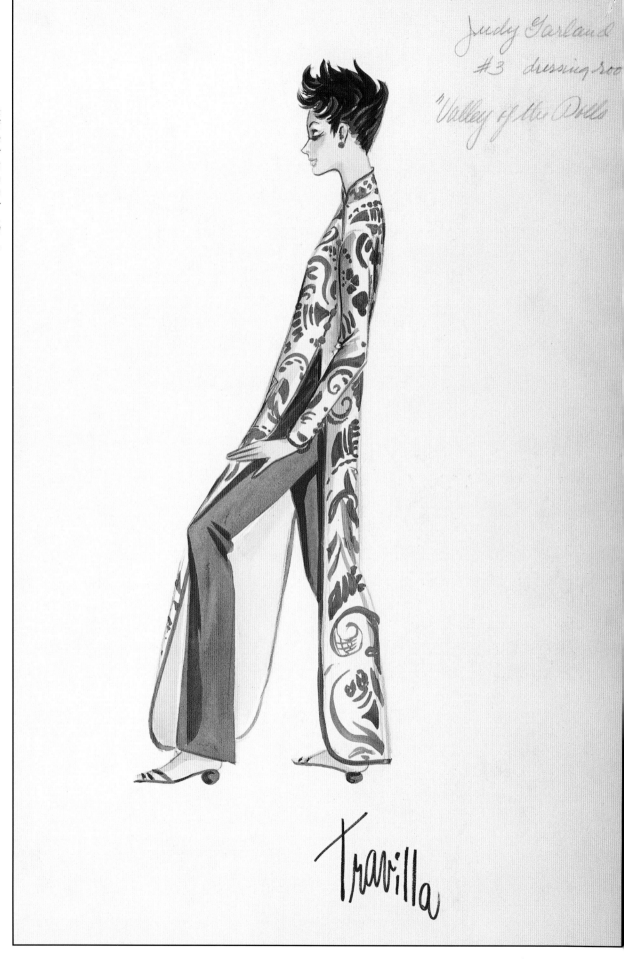

Judy Garland
#3 dressing room
"Valley of the Dolls"

Travilla

When Susan Hayward was cast as a replacement, Travilla re-cut Garland's costumes to fit her. "She made me take everything out—the lining, the pads, everything. That way, she thought she'd look thinner. I argued that the gowns would fall out of shape. In the end I had no choice but to take it all out; only the beads stayed."

The female cast was rounded out by Barbara Parkins as the small town girl who makes it big in Manhattan. Travilla designed a bevy of dreamy gowns for her fling as a cosmetics spokesmodel, which plays like a fashion show in the middle of the movie.

Fitting a gown on Parkins for her modeling bit in *Dolls*. *Collection of Bill Sarris.*

This sketch shows a hot pink flounce-hem mini designed for Barbara Parkins. Only the white-beaded daisy bodice is visible in the movie. In the publicity still, Travilla poses with Parkins and Tate. *Collection of Bill Sarris.*

"VALLEY OF THE DOLLS

Barbara Parkins
#5
montage sc

Travilla

An innocently sexy
pink baby-doll dress,
worn by Parkins in
the fashion segment.
*Collection of Bill
Sarris.*

Parkins wore this ribbed wool mocha coat early in the film. *Collection of Bill Sarris.*

ANNE

Tag Sc.

Ext Anne's House

Travilla

Yet another coat for Parkins. Graphic black and white plaid was a strong element of 1960s style. *Collection of Bill Sarris.*

The double-breasted leopard coat designed for Parkins. (A single-breasted version was worn by Patty Duke.) *Collection of Bill Sarris.*

Hayward belts out a Broadway tune, dazzling in a high-wattage Travilla gown of beaded soufflé. *Academy of Motion Picture Arts and Sciences.*

A camel coat for the delicate Sharon Tate, belted for a slim empire silhouette. *Collection of Bill Sarris.*

Travilla, surrounded by sketchboards—most of which are for *Valley of the Dolls. Collection of Bill Sarris.*

WUSA (1969)

A reality movie in which Paul Newman and Joanne Woodward struggle to keep their ratings high at the radio station WUSA.

Joanne Woodward is cool and sophisticated in a white wool crepe after-five dress and a melon silk shirtdress. *Collection of Bill Sarris.*

Looking natty, Paul Newman wears a traditional double-breasted navy blue blazer and a trendsetting three-button glen plaid suit. *Collection of Bill Sarris.*

Cabo Blanco (1979)

Charles Bronson plays a tough guy in tropical Cabo Blanco. He was a nightclub owner whose thin veneer of civilization covers a wild past.

Travilla didn't think of Cabo Blanco as a design challenge. "From my point of view," he said, "there were no great clothes required." Instead, it was a personal challenge, given a run-in with the male lead.

Travilla, relaxing on location in Mexico with members of the Cabo Blanco cast. Collection of Bill Sarris.

"Cabo Blanco
Charles Bronson
#3 Int. Club

The beautiful pants in this costume were unappreciated by Charles Bronson. *Collection of Bill Sarris.*

Travilla

"One of my worst experiences was designing for Charles Bronson in *Cabo Blanco*," he said. "The scene was set in 1940, and he played a macho role. He would have worn rough clothes like Levis and open-neck cotton shirts. But there was a nightclub where he needed slacks and a jacket, and that's where the trouble started."

Travilla found Bronson vain and demanding. "He had a great body, and the idea was to show it. That was easy to achieve with Levis, with a snug fit, but not quite so easy with the loose pants of the period. Still, I managed to cut him the most beautiful pair of pants," he recalled. "They were so beautiful, I would have loved to have had a pair like that myself."

Years later, Travilla could still remember the design in great detail. "What I did was to closely fit the back of the pants from seam-to-seam and across the back. Then I put an inside lining from seam-to-seam across the front, to control the outer pleats.

"It made the slacks fall as if on a hanger, but you could still see his ass! Even the darts on the buttocks were on the bias, and the crotch line was traced inward so it followed his contour without being vulgar."

Bronson's wife, Jill Ireland, was present for a fitting and she told him: "Those are the most beautiful pants I've ever seen on you." His response was to growl: "I hate 'em."

149

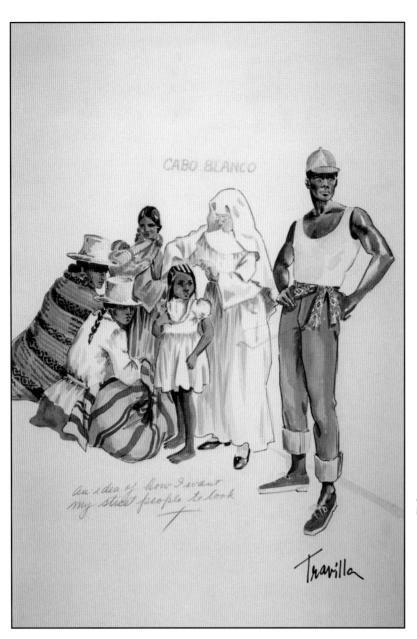

CABO BLANCO

An idea of how I want
my street people to look

Travilla

A unique group sketch for *Cabo Blanco. Collection of
Bill Sarris.*

In another incident, Travilla purchased dozens of workshirts
and blue jeans for Bronson to try on, ranging in cost from
$12.00 to $125.00. "I had Levis stacked up on the floor, also
shirts, and all these things had come from the stores.

"Bronson came in, took a look at something, and said he
didn't like it. Then he kicked it! But he had just come in from
the street and his feet were dirty. I had to pay for those things
he didn't like," Travilla revealed.

"He was abusive. I think he was living up to his macho
image." Fair to a fault, when Travilla saw the final version of
Cabo Blanco he admired Bronson's persona. "My god, he does
look good up there on screen!"

Travilla did not find these peasant costumes
challenging. By way of contrast, he took pride in
designing more rugged and authentic peasant
attire for *Viva Zapata!* Collection of Bill Sarris.

Travilla's black ballgown with white bandeau top and Watteau train as sketched, and as worn by Loretta Young. Collection of Bill Sarris.

Chapter Seven

Television Style

Travilla freelanced for the television industry throughout the 1970s and 1980s. As with the movies, there are gaps in the extant sketches and photos, which are presented here to the extent available.

The Loretta Young Show (1950s)

Each week, Loretta Young opened the door to glamour when she swirled onto the set of her TV show. She emceed a series of dramas, promoted by the makers of a boxed laundry soap that she carried in her manicured hands.

"I really enjoyed *The Loretta Young Show*, possibly because Loretta was such an elegant lady and so easy to design for. Everything looked good on her. She was also truly appreciative of good clothing design," Travilla said. "Working with her was a piece of heaven."

Travilla found in Young ". . . one of those rare ladies who, even if she didn't care for the dress, could understand it." As he explained: "There were so many clothes we had to put on her, but I'd explain conceptually what I was doing and she would understand. She enjoyed being different each week."

Travilla also respected her ability to critique herself, in a detached manner. "She could put a dress on and stand in front of the mirror and say: 'You know, Bill, I would never wear this but maybe Loretta Young would.'"

A variety of the entrance-making gowns designed by Travilla for *The Loretta Young Show*. Collection of Bill Sarris.

Loretta Young

*Dear Bill —
aren't you
darling to —
me such a
note — I'm so th*

You enjoyed the show.
I certainly did love making it – When the part is there its like rolling off a log – Easy & fun –

You have my deepest affection always – as you must know by now –

Thanks again for being so thoughtful
Loretta

This charming thank-you note was penned by Young.

Evita Peron (1981)

This made-for-TV movie was about Eva Peron, who rose from a humble birth to become the wife of Argentine leader Juan Peron. Faye Dunaway was cast as the humbly-born Evita, wildly popular as the first lady of Argentina—despite her flamboyant lifestyle and international reputation for dressing extravagantly. Fortunately, almost all of Travilla's sketches for Dunaway have survived.

Travilla put Faye Dunaway into sixty-three costume changes for the television special *Evita Peron*. He also outfitted James Farentino with thirty-six changes for his role as the dapper Juan Peron. To accomplish this, Travilla had two departments sewing—five tailors and five seamstresses—and used seven wardrobe assistants.

In terms of sheer volume, it was the biggest assignment Travilla had tackled yet. "I've never worked so hard in my life," he said. "I had the dressmakers working just 10 minutes ahead of a scene. Eva Peron used to spend $50,000 for a single dress, so I couldn't cheat on the clothing."

It was a tough role for the actress due to the tempestuous nature of the character she was playing, and this difficulty translated into fitting problems for Travilla—particularly as filming progressed.

It started out well enough, when he flew to New York for an interview at Dunaway's penthouse apartment overlooking Central Park. This despite the fact that she already had costume designers with whom she usually insisted on working. "I took the elevator to the top floor and stepped out into a foyer to find the three remaining walls covered with framed sketches by her two favorite designers.

"I thought to myself, 'Oh hell! I'm dead. She likes them so much she is never going to have time for me.' But I was determined that I would at least show her my drawings," he said. "I wanted to work on the series; it was a wonderful showcase for clothes."

Fortunately, Dunaway was delighted with the sample sketches he brought to the interview. They met for three hours, and Travilla was looking forward to their next meeting. That's when the trouble started—over a gray gabardine suit.

"I had sketched it for her in advance and at the time she had liked it. Then she phoned me and said the suit was too modern, it didn't fit the period. But I knew it did because what I had done—it was cheating in a sense—was to make exactly the same suit as I had made for a film when I was at Fox, in 1949! I knew it was the period, it was smart then and still smart today."

But Dunaway was adamant in rejecting his sketch of the gray suit. Travilla realized he would just have to convince her otherwise, since it was already being made. "The suit is right on period, and I'll send you a wardrobe still of the exact same suit I made in 1949. I'm insisting this is the way you look, instead of being foolishly overdressed." he told her.

The darker gray suit is a costume designed by Travilla in the 1940s. Compare it to the similar style that he adapted twenty years later for *Evita*. *Collection of Bill Sarris.*

Travilla

Travilla engineered an allover petal skirt for this ballgown.
Collection of Bill Sarris.

"She got the still, she gave in, and she apologized." Having jumped that designing hurdle, Travilla found there were others.

"Faye was still sweet, thoughtful and very businesslike," he recalled. "But I noticed she was not quite as friendly as she had been in New York." Apparently, she was a workaholic who insisted on all-day fittings and constant alterations to the costumes.

"She would tell the tailor she wanted her jacket a quarter of an inch shorter in the front because it wasn't even. He was ready to put a chalk mark on the cloth, the way a tailor works. But she said he must 'turn it up.' Well, you can't turn up that amount of fabric, with the facing and everything."

At other times, Dunaway would assault the staff milliner with minute instructions about the placement of a dimple in a beret. As Travilla put it: "Faye was a very tough lady and each day she got tougher." Finally, she blew up at him on the set when he attempted to adjust the drape of a fox stole across her shoulders.

A lilac walking suit with peplum detail. Note the saucily tilted beret, a favorite headgear for Dunaway.
Collection of Bill Sarris.

Travilla

Travilla was ready to walk off the show, but the director talked him out of it. "He told me we had the same problem, that it was no longer Faye Dunaway shooting a movie, it was Eva Peron. 'She becomes more like that woman every day,' he said. 'But Bill, she's magnificent.'

"I can't blame Faye. She *was* Evita Peron and she lived it, and she never let her real life come through. She was difficult but [it was] worthwhile. Faye not only wears my costumes beautifully, she becomes the character and is glorious in those clothes."

Black military frogs balance the boldness of black fur sleeves on this extravagant daytime suit. *Collection of Bill Sarris.*

Variations on a theme—Travilla made two sketches of the same soft gray suit with tunic jacket. *Collection of Bill Sarris.*

More gray notes for Evita, sporty in two-tone and dressy with a bowed jabot detail.

And for country, a sophisticated woolen set in cream and camel. *Collection of Bill Sarris.*

Two camel suitings, just right for town. *Collection of Bill Sarris.*

This gold lace peignoir sets a romantic scene. *Collection of Bill Sarris.*

Opposite page, bottom left: Why not a gray suit for evening, when it's in ribbed silk with a velvet collar? *Collection of Bill Sarris.*

Bottom right: A male counterfoil to the impetuous Evita in the role played by James Farentino. *Collection of Bill Sarris.*

The Thorn Birds (1983)

Based on the popular book by Carson McCulloch, this is the story of a large family trying to eke out a living on a sheep ranch in Australia, which they stand to inherit from a tough businesswoman played by Barbara Stanwyck. The saga begins in the 1910s and continues for two decades. Also stars Richard Chamberlain as a Catholic priest who had a brief affair with the daughter, played by Rachel Ward.

The Thorn Birds was a mini-series that gave Travilla ample time to work out his design concepts, a welcome relief from the pressures of *Dallas* (see page 171). "It was a beautiful story of passion and grief with wonderful characters, and I had the time to chat with the actors about their scenes, and establish the moods."

Travilla was charged with showing cleavage on ingénue Rachel Ward, but since that was unheard of in the 1920s, he cut her necklines as low as he dared. "I had to fit her clothes a little bit differently, stepping a shade out of period, and I cut her necklines half an inch lower than what they truly would have been.

"In those days women didn't want to be women," Travilla complained. "They wore bandages and bound their breasts to crush them flat, to create a boyish look —which is dumb!"

Travilla played a similar trick in the non-clerical costumes for Richard Chamberlain as Father Ralph de Bricassart. "There were times when he needed to be portrayed as this handsome, attractive man embroiled in a passionate and forbidden love affair.

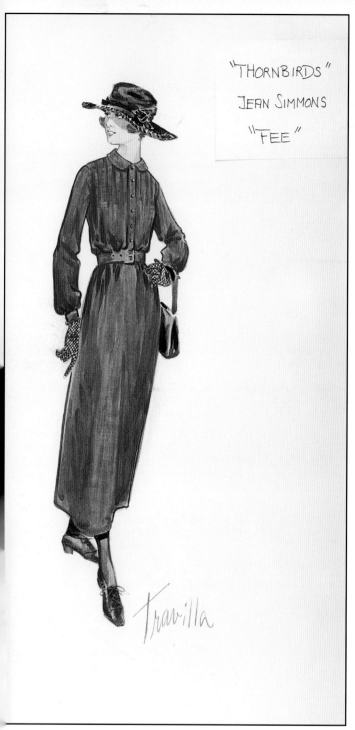

Jean Simmons in a classic walking suit. *Collection of Bill Sarris.*

An Alice-blue chiffon gown for the role of Mrs. Quirk. *Collection of Bill Sarris.*

Opposite page: On the set with Stanwyck, who Travilla admired for her professional attitude. *Collection of Bill Sarris.*

"My job was to bring out the sensual side of him for the camera. To effect this, I put Richard in boots and jodhpurs and I gave him very fine, thin cotton shirts. But I cut them on the bias.

"Richard's shirts were regular shirts of the period," he said. "There were no changes in the pattern, just the grain of fabric. But because I cut them on the bias, they were sexy shirts—you could see his body right through them."

Travilla especially enjoyed working with Barbara Stanwyck, who was seventy-five at the time of filming. "She had the figure of a child, a waist of 25-1/2 inches. She was trim, erect, alive and youthful," he recalled. "She was a lesson to everyone. Always professional, if she had to be on the set at 9:00 a.m. she would be there in full makeup, dressed in costume and ready to work at 8:45 a.m."

Mrs Quirk

Mary Carson
#7
with Lawyer

Travilla

Elegant clothing helped define the rich matriarch role
played by Barbara Stanwyck.

Barbara Stanwyck
#3
"THORN BIRDS"

Travilla

Mary Carson
4
drawing Room
Arrival of the Clearys
Barbara Stanwyck

Travilla

Travilla relied heavily
on lace to create an
opulent look for
Stanwyck. *Collection
of Bill Sarris.*

The well-endowed Rachel Ward in evening dresses cut as low as Travilla dared. Note the two different sketches of a similar pink chiffon dance dress. *Collection of Bill Sarris.*

Rachael Ward
'Meggie
#6
THORN BIRDS

THORNBIRDS
Meggie

5   sc. 33 - 49
Int. drawingroom
Int. entry Melbourne Hotel
Int. waiting room
Int. Entry Prison
Ext veranda Drogheda

Rachel Ward

Ward's character matured as *The Thorn Birds* progressed, but her décolletage remained low-cut. *Collection of Bill Sarris.*

"THORNBIRDS"
BABARA STANWYCK
"MARY" CARSON

Travilla

Stanwyck's character also matured, growing older but no kinder. Her ensembles declared her a woman of worldly chic. *Collection of Bill Sarris.*

Mary Carson
#8
sc 137 Ext Verauda

Travilla

Julia (1960s)

A popular sitcom starring Diahann Carroll, television's first black star, as a spunky nurse with a stupendous wardrobe.

The pair posed informally at an awards banquet, she in a gown of his design. *Collection of Bill Sarris.*

"I designed the full run of *Julia*, a real favorite because I so enjoyed working with Diahann Carroll," Travilla said. "It was a great challenge for me . . . to make her clothes glamorous in a modern sense, without overlooking the African roots that were a trademark of her show. I finally went on a camera safari in Africa for ideas. The tribal dress was so incredible, it inspired some of my most elegant clothing for my own label."

Tunic time, in persimmon and winter white.
Collection of Bill Sarris.

Front and back views of a "sigh-voltage" white satin evening gown. The diamanté straps add more brilliance. *Collection of Bill Sarris.*

A breathtaking wedding gown imbued with medieval grace. *Collection of Bill Sarris.*

Diahann Carroll
Julia
Sc 73 – 84
Chg # 3

Travilla

Some of Travilla's favorite work was for Diahann Carroll. This white lace gown was designed either for *Julia* or a special event. *Collection of Bill Sarris.*

Dallas (1978–1980s)

The nighttime "soap" that played opposite Dynasty, featuring the lives and loves of a powerful oil-rich family in Dallas. Featuring Larry Hagman, Linda Gray, Susan Howard, Charlene Tilton, Priscilla Presley, Victoria Principal, and Deborah Shelton.

Travilla began designing for *Dallas* in 1978 and won an Emmy the first year for his elegant clothing concept. He'd been brought in to rev up the leading ladies' wardrobes, when Lorimar Productions realized their ratings were taking a hit due to the popularity of Nolan Miller's designs for the rival series *Dynasty*.

"It was a real shock when I picked up my phone one day and my agent said, all excited: 'Lorimar wants you to do *Dallas*!' For one thing, even though it was just about the biggest show on TV at that time, I had never seen it. But I went to an interview

where the producers explained the deadlines. It seemed like an awful lot of work!

"I asked why they were interested in me; they explained that fans were complaining about the clothes." Lorimar wanted a "real Texas rich" look for the show, which Travilla was able to deliver.

"Now, I knew Texas from marketing my own line. They're a little more show-off in Texas. Southern ladies love color, they love to wear their jewelry." Showy or not, the producers explicitly asked Travilla to make *Dallas* look like real life as compared to the larger-than-life appearance of *Dynasty*.

"I thought it could really be a great show, and it would be a challenge for me to bring out the identity of each principal character . . . in wardrobe. Hard work it turned out to be, but I could never resist a challenge," Travilla said.

"The best thing about the show was getting to know the actresses. On a professional level, my goal was to gradually give each one her own identity," he said. "When I first saw the show I thought the girls looked dull, plus they didn't look wealthy. They looked as though they had one big shared wardrobe, of clothes that weren't too well-made."

His first job was to create separate fashion identities for each of the stars. "I tried to give Linda Gray more sensual, feminine clothing; I tried to keep Victoria Principal more European, very Italian." Travilla also explained his theory that the character played by Priscilla Presley would have many changes and good accessories, since she owned a boutique on the show. For Susan Howard, he emphasized the character's political background in clothes that were a bit crisper and more tailored.

Travilla, posing with a star in bridal costume. Collection of Bill Sarris.

The Beautiful Linda

As Travilla worked with the cast members, they often became friends. He was especially close to Linda Gray, who was "not only beautiful and talented, but truly thoughtful." At one point, he and Gray crossed travel routes during his promotional trip to London for a Dallas-inspired clothing line.

Gray was prompted her to pen an ebullient message on her private, gray-tinted stationery: "My dear darling dirty old man," she wrote, "...I'm off to do a talk show with Larry in Paris and then on to Milan to see some of the collections! Whee— what fun! How we got out of filming for a week I don't know but hell—I'm going anyway! Can't wait to see you and your new collection which I know must be divine!"

Sketched for Linda Gray, a black cascade of tulle with black-tipped white maribou trimmings. *Collection of Bill Sarris.*

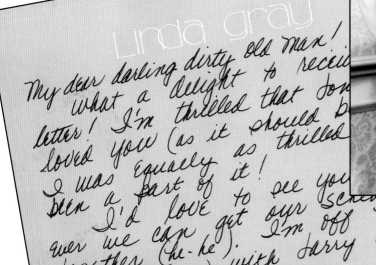

With Linda Gray, one of his closest friends from *Dallas*. She models the same black column of tulle and sequins to great advantage, in a publicity photo. *Collection of Bill Sarris.*

Linda Gray

My dear darling dirty old man!
What a delight to recei[ve]
letter! I'm thrilled that [you]
loved you (as it should b[e]
I was equally as thrilled
been a part of it!
I'd love to see you
ever we can get our sche[dules]
together (he-he). I'm off to do
[a talk] show with *Larry* in Paris

[a]nd then on to Milan to see
some of the collections!
Whee — what fun! How we
got out of filming for a
week I don't know but
hell — I'm going anyway!!!
Can't wait to see you
and your new collection which
I know must be divine!!
Big Hugs
Linda
xxoo

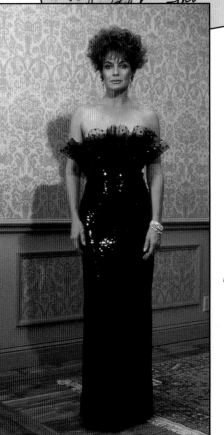

Gray liked to tease Travilla, as seen in her note to "My dear darling dirty old man!" *Collection of Bill Sarris.*

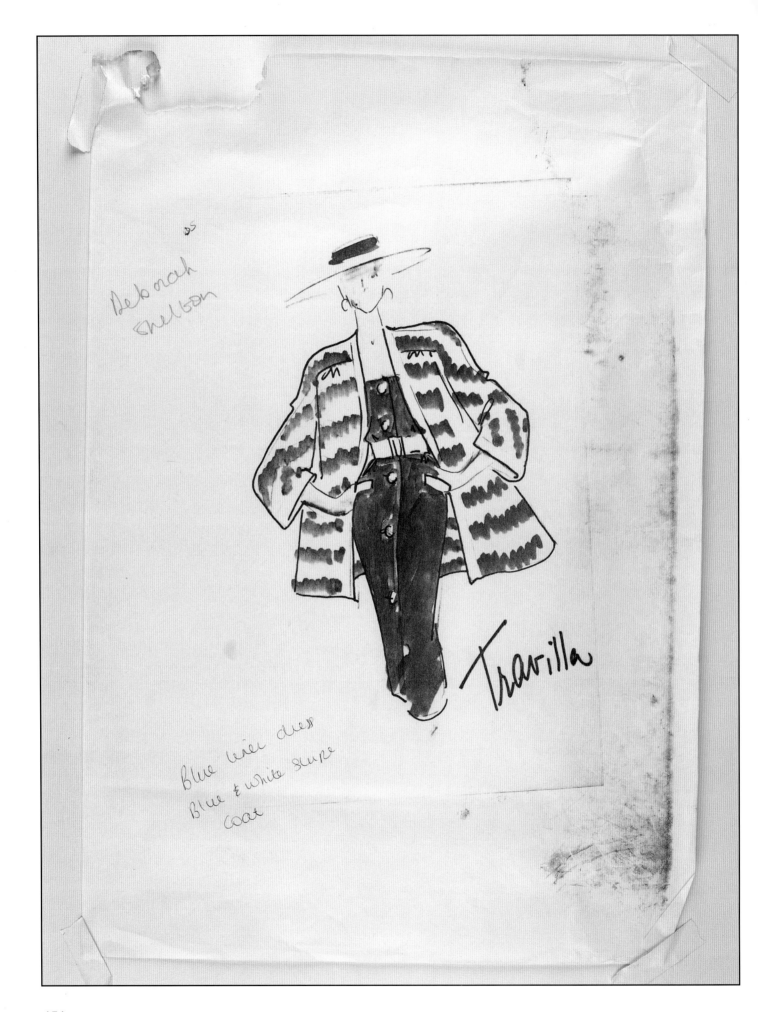

as
Deborah
Shelton

Travilla

Blue linen dress
Blue & white stripe
coat

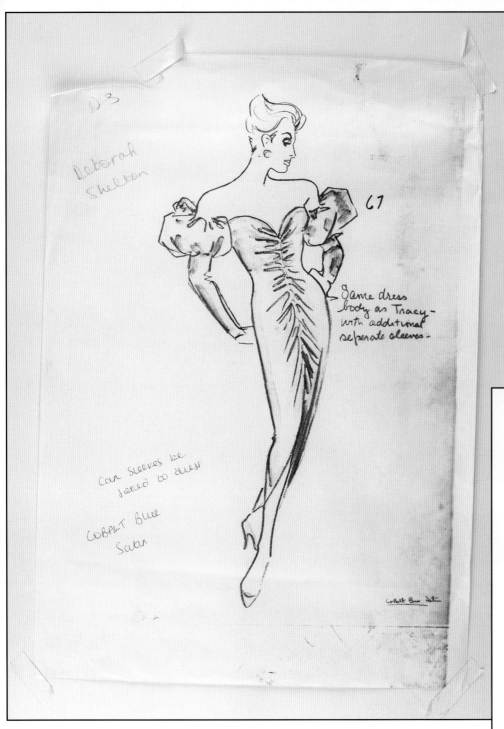

The tissue sketch of a disco dress comes to life when Shelton preens in the actual creation. *Collection of Bill Sarris.*

Opposite page: A simple working sketch on tissue paper of a daytime ensemble in blue and white linen, for Deborah Shelton. *Collection of Bill Sarris.*

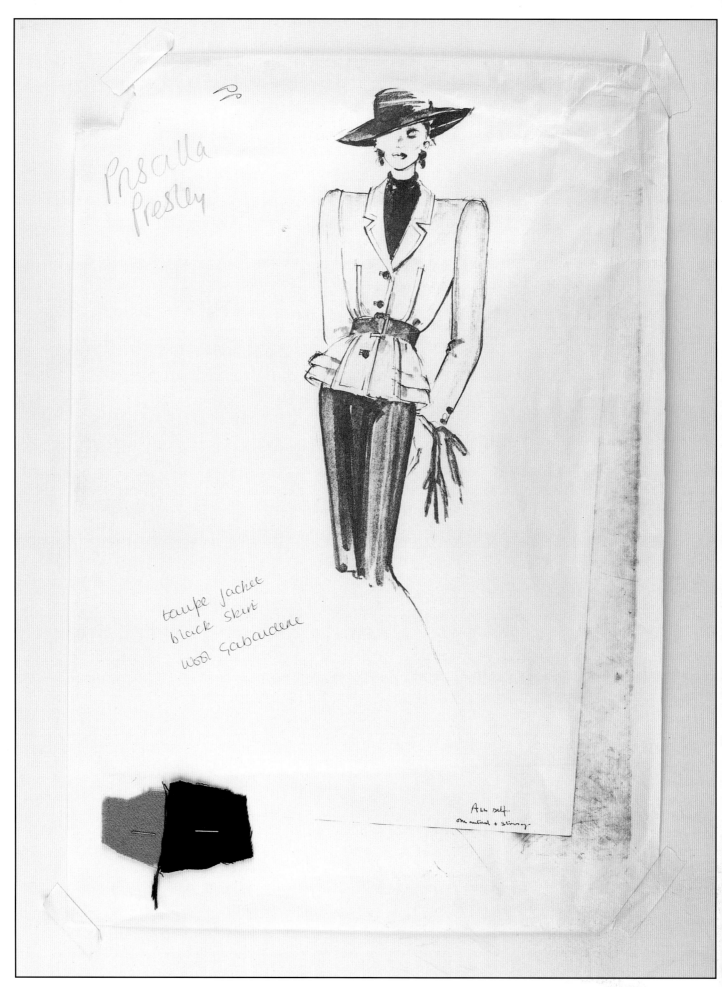

Prisalla
Presley

taupe Jacket
black skirt
wool Gabaudene

All self.
the natural + strongy.

More working sketches, for Priscilla Presley. The wool gabardine suit for day features a peplum jacket.
The cocktail suit is in navy lace and taffeta. *Collection of Bill Sarris.*

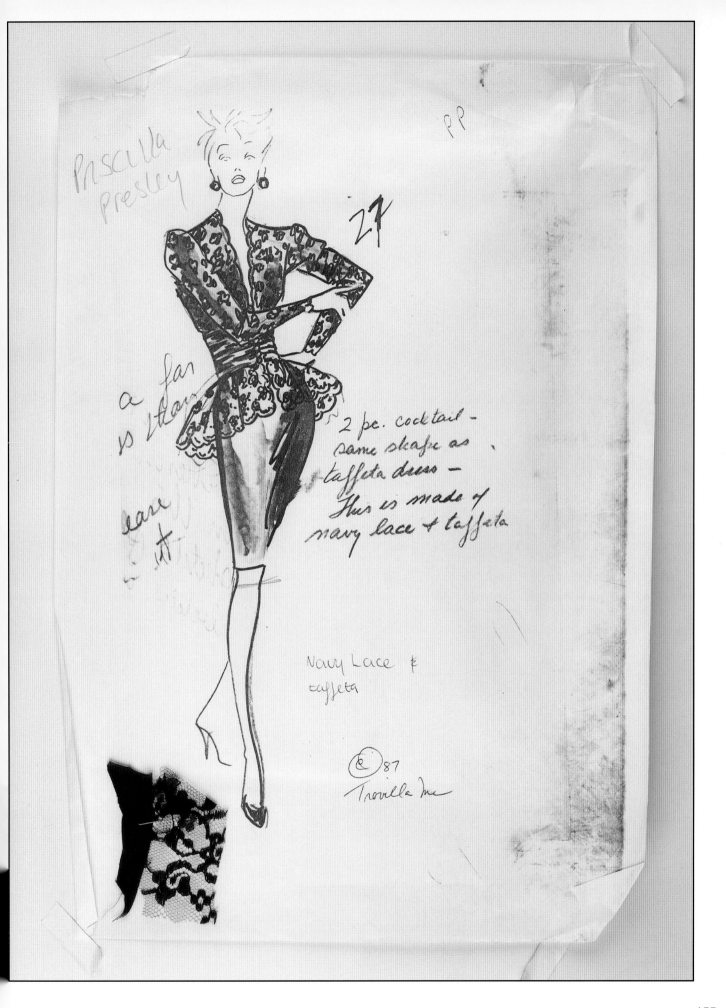

Priscilla Presley

P.P.

PP

a far
is than

2 pc. cocktail -
same shape as
taffeta dress -
This is made of
navy lace & taffeta

Navy Lace &
taffeta

© 87
Travilla Inc

Gray is resplendent in red velvet and a regal satin-backed stole. Travilla liked to use strong colors on Gray, as a match for her character's strength. *Collection of Bill Sarris.*

This evening gown,
modeled by Barbara
Carrera, was designed
for *Dallas*. Collection
of Bill Sarris.

The *Dallas* Clothing Line

He stayed with *Dallas* for two seasons, to great acclaim. In fact, Travilla's success on the series led him to expand his business. "My clothes were seen immediately, every week, all over the world," he said. "Lorimar began getting requests from fans who wanted to buy the same clothes. That inspired a whole new collection for me."

When accepting any freelance work, Travilla considered his own clothing business first—and this was no

Travilla, during the
Dallas years.
Collection of Bill Sarris.

exception. In negotiating his contract with Lorimar, he insisted on the right to adapt any costume designs. He easily reached a broad market with the Dallas-inspired line. Unlike his private-label collection, these clothes were priced within reach of the average consumer, and they spread his style influence far and wide.

"I even marketed overseas, through the *Littlewoods* catalog published in London."

Travilla and the stars of *Dallas* had become friends, and many of them—including Barbara Carrera, Priscilla Presley, and Linda Gray—agreed to model his line for the catalog.

Two ways to shine at night. The captivating cocktail dress features a rose-trimmed scoop neck and a demi-train hemline. The disco dress is vibrant in raspberry sequins with a black tulle handkerchief skirt. *Collection of Bill Sarris.*

Emma Sands modeled this purple wool crepe suit for the Littlewoods catalog. *Collection of Bill Sarris.*

Travilla once put Marilyn Monroe in a white terrycloth robe for a bathtub scene in *The Seven Year Itch*. Here, a luxury version in pink for his *Dallas*-based catalog line. *Collection of Bill Sarris.*

Author's Notes

It was in the course of researching *California Couture*, a study of that state's legacy of high-end designers, that I stumbled across an amazing collection of original costume sketches by the late Bill Travilla. Dozens of these sketches, along with photos and other memorabilia, were stored rather haphazardly in a small, dusty loft upstairs from the workrooms at *Travilla, Inc.*

It turned out that Bill Sarris, Travilla's longtime friend and partner, had preserved everything he could after a devastating fire swept through a prior location. He also had notes and press clippings for the memoirs that Travilla had been planning to publish at the time of his unexpected death in 1990.

There had been many magazine and newspaper interviews of Travilla, especially in Los Angeles, in connection with his clothing collections. However, not much had been written about the breadth of his work in the movie and television industry. Apparently, Travilla was rather shy, and avoided the limelight of Hollywood with its public relations machinery. The concept of this book, therefore, is to chronicle what has been preserved of his career in costume design, primarily by providing a showcase for the extant sketches.

An elegantly subdued gown for the role of Lee (formerly Helen), from an unknown production in the 1960s. *Collection of Bill Sarris.*

Adriana
sc #113
Int Winthrop lib
sc 153 - 163

Travilla

What is so charming about these sketches is their detail, and their painterly quality. It's the same quality that drew Sonja Henie and Ann Sheridan to Travilla early in his career; and made lifelong fans of such stars as Marilyn Monroe, Loretta Young, Diahann Carroll, Sharon Tate, and Linda Gray.

Lisa
#19
Int Wintrop Library sc 304

Sharon Tate

Travilla

Travilla found Sharon Tate as beautiful in her personality as in her person. They worked together on *Valley of the Dolls* (1967) and at least one other production, for which he produced these sketches.
Collection of Bill Sarris.

The sketches stand on their own as art, the product of Travilla's early training in sculpture and painting. They reflect his eye for detail and color harmony, which I've tried to bring out in the chapter on "Design Theory." But the sketches don't do justice to his unique talent as an *engineer* of clothing.

Driven by the exigencies of costume design, Travilla learned to camouflage flaws and enhance characterization through wiring, bonding, and draping. His favorite cut was on the bias, because it allowed fabric to flow with the body. His favorite technique was pleating, because it gave movement to a silhouette.

A 1950s sketch for a costume (production unknown).

Sadly, much information has already been lost about the movies, TV shows, and special appearances that Travilla worked on—especially because costume designers often fail to receive serious recognition. I elected to include some sketches that appear to be for costumes or special events, even though the production was unknown.

What *was* available has been preserved in this book, and I can only hope that it pays adequate tribute to one of the great designers of the past century.

With many thanks to Bill Sarris, and to staff at the Margaret Herrick Library in the Academy for Motion Picture Arts and Sciences. And a special thank you to Nancy Schiffer, who believed this book was possible.

Costume sketches for the role of Cathy Palmer, circa 1969 (production unknown). *Collection of Bill Sarris.*

The feather bodice on this extravagant ballgown would have required boning, or some other form of the "engineering" for which Travilla was so well-known. *Collection of Bill Sarris.*

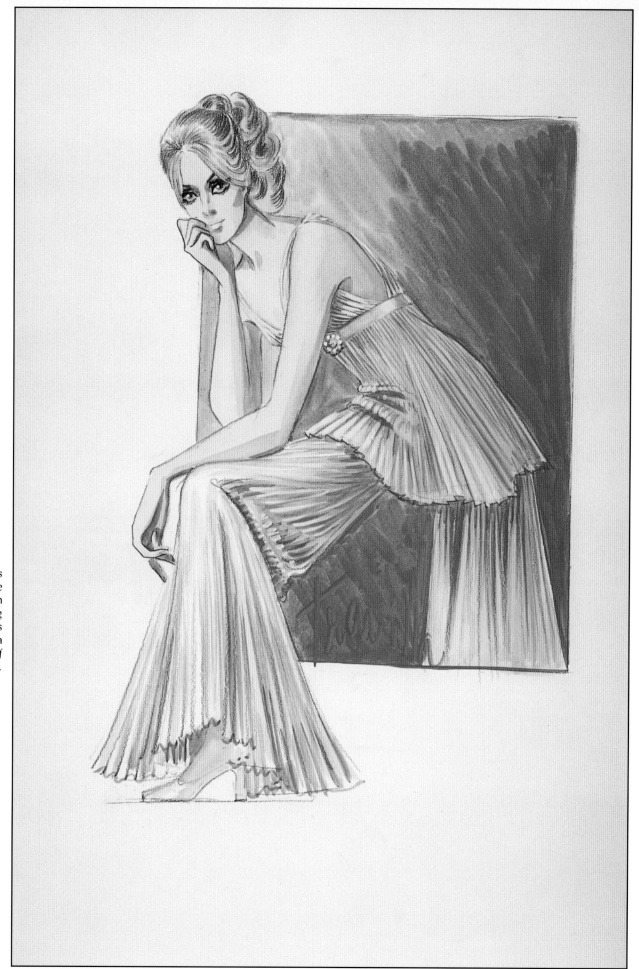

Travilla was famous for his innovative use of pleats, as seen in these evening pajamas from his private label, circa 1970. *Collection of Bill Sarris.*

More pleating, in a mini-dress circa 1965. Collection of Bill Sarris.

Fabulous vermicelli-beaded
evening pants, circa 1980.
Travilla often used Hollywood
costume techniques such as
this, in his own line. *Collection
of Bill Sarris.*

Bibliography

Bold, Kathryn. "A Fashion Show for the Man Who Dressed Marilyn Monroe." *Los Angeles Times*. September 7, 1990.

Brown, Les, ed. *New York Times Encyclopedia of Television*. New York City: Times Books, 1977.

Chierichetti, David. *Hollywood Costume Design*. New York City: Harmony Books (Crown), 1976.

Conway, Michael, and Mark Ricci, eds. *The Films of Marilyn Monroe*. Secaucus, NJ: The Citadel Press, 1973.

Dorantes, Gayle. "The News in Acapulco." *The News World Soccer Cup Supplement* (Mexico City). June 7, 1970.

Garlow, Jean. Interview with the author August 13, 2001.

Houston-Montgomery, Beauregard. "Travilla." *Interview*. July 1986.

Johnson, Erskine. "Designer Slaps at Dowdy Stars." *Los Angeles Mirror*. August 25, 1961.

Karanikas, Diana. *Marilyn: A Life In Pictures*. New York City: Metro Books, 1991.

Kellin, Dana. "Travilla: Remembering Marilyn." *W*. March 19-26, 1990.

___. "Lavish Wardrobe for Faye." *TV Week*. February 22-28, 1981.

Leese, Elizabeth. *Costume Design in the Movies*. New York City: Dover Publications, Inc., 1991.

Lilliston, Lynn. "William Travilla Suits the Stars." *Los Angeles Times*. September 12, 1968.

Mann, Arnold. "Top of the Line Design." *Emmy Magazine*. March/April 1984.

Moses, Robert, ed. *AMC Classic Movie Companion*. New York: Hyperion, 1999.

___. *New York Times Film Reviews*. New York City: N.Y. Times & Arno Press, 1970.

Reilly, Maureen. *California Couture*. Atglen, PA: Schiffer Publishing Ltd., 2000.

Rourke, Mary. "Stars in His Eyes." *Los Angeles Times*. October 23, 1981.

Russell, Sue. "The Man Who's Putting the Dazzle Into Dallas." *Woman*. February 8, 1986.

Sarris, Bill. Interviews with the author in June and December, 2000; May and August, 2001.